THE VILLAGE WAY

Educating Towards a Life of Meaning

Dotan Levi

CENTRAL PARK SOUTH PUBLISHING

Published by Central Park South Publishing 2022
www.centralparksouthpublishing.com

Typesetting and e-book formatting services by Victor Marcos

ISBN:
978-1-956452-23-5 (hbk)
978-1-956452-24-2 (pbk)
978-1-956452-25-9 (ebk)

Table of Contents

Author's Note

This book, originally published in Hebrew in 2018, was written before the onset of the coronavirus pandemic. In the stories on the following pages, readers will surely notice the lack of reference to the many issues, challenges, and educational opportunities that have come up during this time.

The pandemic affected all of our lives in many ways, and has certainly had an impact on teenagers and educators. With all that has happened, one could ask—is this book still relevant?

I will share with you just one of the things that we have seen change in our work with educators over these past few years. Before the pandemic, when we at the Village Way Educational Institute would come to a school for the first time, we would talk about the important role that a school needs to play in the social, emotional, and ethical development of their students. Back then, this idea was sometimes met with resistance; not all educators believed that they had any educational responsibilities beyond teaching the material and striving towards academic excellence.

Now, in the wake of the pandemic, it is widely recognized that the educational function of a school goes far beyond how students perform on tests. Once the experience of attending school in person was taken away from so many, everyone became acutely aware of the importance of the social and emotional aspects of the school experience. This has reinforced our mission of empowering educators and educational communities with a value-driven methodology to guide this educational work.

Benjamin Franklin said: "Either write something worth reading or do something worth writing." As I reflect on the writing of this book, I find myself asking: Have I written something worth reading? I do not know, but of one thing, I am sure. I am certain that the thousands of educators who are with us in the Village Way are doing something worth writing about.

—Dotan Levi, March 2022

Preface

It takes a village to raise a child, and it takes a supportive adult to believe in them. It also requires understanding that the young person seeks meaning in life. These are the three basic principles that underlie the Village Way educational philosophy, a comprehensive approach that includes methods and best practices used to help adolescents develop into adults who are capable of contributing to and influencing the society in which they live.

The Village Way is used by thousands of educators in dozens of educational communities throughout Israel. It was developed over many years by founder Dr. Chaim Peri and the educators who worked with him at Yemin Orde Youth Village. They have perfected and adapted educational methods that scholars conceived of many years earlier. Although many of the components of the philosophy will be familiar to educators, and every parent can identify some to which he or she ascribes, the innovation in the Village Way is that these concepts have been transformed into accessible tools. These tools generate an educational environment that helps parents nurture their children and allows educators at schools and other institutions to find a common language, skills and programs to meet the challenge to which they have devoted their lives.

We chose to present the Village Way methodology through the story of Dotan Levi, who has educated adolescents in various frameworks and has spent many years working alongside Dr. Chaim. Today, as head of the Village Way Educational Institute, he leads the development of this philosophy and its dissemination throughout Israel.

Both parents and educators experience discomfort in their encounters with kids. We can all recall the confusion, frustration, and helplessness that can happen because of a comment or behavior that we may not have the tools to decipher. This book offers direction and a way to help us become more supportive parents, educators, and people.

The Village Way is an educational philosophy that is suitable for every place where people live and work together as a family unit and any educational framework with students of any age. For ideological reasons, we choose to work with educational communities that serve youth at-risk in the social and geographic periphery of Israeli society.

The Village Way philosophy is the work of many individuals. It is alive and well in the field, and thankfully, is being developed and improved upon by many educators who share it throughout the country: Muslims, Druze, and Christians; secular and traditional Jews, as well as modern Orthodox and ultra-Orthodox educators in youth villages[1], high schools, and other educational communities. This book belongs to them, educators who work both day and night helping young men and women who can now look forward to a better future. We believe that education leads society and that educators are nation-builders, worthy of our gratitude and blessings.

We have been privileged to publish this Village Way book thanks to the determination, devotion, and professionalism of all the staff members at the Village Way Educational Institute, the *mechina* gap-year leadership programs, and the resource development, finance, and logistics departments. I want to express appreciation to our partners in Israel and abroad, headed by our dear friends from ImpactIsrael, formerly known as Friends of Yemin Orde. We invite you to join us on a fascinating educational journey with the Village Way.

—Haim Rubovitch, Founding CEO, *Village Way Educational Initiatives*

---

1 Youth villages: residential educational communities for adolescents that combine formal and informal education. The concept and term originated in Israel.

Introduction

The Test Lesson

Years spent as a youth movement counselor and studying toward a BA and teaching certificate, followed by months spent teaching Bible and Jewish Law, made me believe that I was more than adequately prepared for being observed by a national inspector while teaching a test lesson—a rite of passage which every new teacher in Israel must go through to receive a permanent teacher's license. On a wintry Sunday morning, the inspector and school principal arrived to observe my lesson. I had come prepared. The lesson plan included objectives and methods, and I envisioned how the blackboard would look at the end. I provided the inspector with my lesson plan and took my place at the front of the classroom. I started by introducing the guest to the students and explained that it is part of the country's responsibility to train teachers, ensuring that they are worthy of investing in Israel's largest national resource—its students. The silence and the looks on their faces told me they understood I was referring to them. Yet despite this auspicious beginning, a moment later, Sarah, a girl who sat at the front of the classroom, jumped up and overturned her desk, shouting a string of curses and insults, including some referring to my mother. Not only did the desk fall on my foot, which was extremely painful, but I was also embarrassed, confused, and insulted. Luckily, she stormed out of the room on the heels of her outburst. I

remember the moment clearly, the physical pain alongside a sense of
helplessness. To this day, I wonder why no one prepared me, or other
new educators, for a moment like this.

In the Israeli military, every combat mission is preceded by a briefing, followed by a review of possible scenarios, and ending with the commander saying: "You always have to expect the unexpected, the scenarios even we cannot predict for you." But what do you do when during your test lesson a student lashes out, flips over her desk and curses? Today, my choices for responding to the outburst are a little clearer to me, but the fact remains that there is no one exact, rehearsed solution for such an event. Teachers and educators, and certainly parents, know their students or children better than any facilitator or lecturer, so the right way for an educator to respond at such a moment—whether ignoring her and continuing with class or stopping the lesson and addressing her—must be theirs to choose.

Professionalism and Authenticity

We know our young people, but we need to deepen our relationship with them as well as improve our ability to see them in new ways. We also know ourselves, and are mostly aware of our strengths and weaknesses, but these too need to be investigated further as we become aware of our automatic behavior, which does not always reflect our intentions. As educators and parents, we are well-versed in the behavior of young people and how we respond based on our own experience; yet it is important to review case studies and take in new ideas based on the experience of colleagues, thus broadening our perspective. In this way, we can improve our intuition, which is a key component in our educational authenticity *and* our professionalism.

Educators must be authentic. An inauthentic educator does not 'pass the test.' All people develop sensors which help us determine if the person standing before us is genuine, whether he is acting in our best interest or has ulterior motives. These sensors weaken over time. During adolescence, they are at their height. Teenagers are sensitive to phony behavior and will refuse to commit to a process guided by someone who wears the mask of a teacher but does not truly embody the educational mission. To lead an educational process, we need to be honest, both with ourselves and with the teens. If we do not really care about them, then, at best, we can only impart knowledge and nothing more.

When Authenticity and Professionalism Collide

In the name of authenticity, one may try to justify inappropriate behavior. The statement: "I am so disappointed in you," might accurately reflect how we feel as a parent or teacher in a situation, but it is harsh and unprofessional. Some would characterize such a statement as 'telling it like it is,' and letting the child deal with reality, but we believe it does more harm than good. Similarly, a teacher or a parent may respond to a teenager with verbal or physical violence and try to justify it by saying, "That's who I am." However, in our view, authenticity, however important, must be tempered by ethical and legal professionalism.

In theory, professionalism and authenticity appear to be opposites, but this is not necessarily the case. What is needed is a flexible method, which both offers an organized framework and allows each person to find their own natural way. The more we practice, the more we can close the gap between our need to be professional and our wish to be authentic.

Why Do We Need a Holistic Educational Philosophy?

A holistic educational philosophy is not a top priority for individual parents and educators. However, for educational communities—schools and youth villages[2]—such a philosophy has great significance. The period of adolescence is a brief window of opportunity in which we can make a dramatic change in a teenager's life. Such a change, when it happens over the course of a limited amount of time, sometimes seems like a miracle; however, it does not happen

---

2   Created in Israel, this is a residential educational environment for youth-at-risk, which includes formal education as well as informal educational, therapeutic services and activities. The idea is to create a cohesive, values-oriented community that provides a safe environment for healthy development, especially for youth who come from challenging backgrounds.

on its own. It requires careful, conscious planning, guidance and perseverance, and even when we make every effort, success is not always guaranteed.

In many educational communities, not enough thought is dedicated to mapping out the ever-changing characteristics of the student population. In fact, sometimes no effort is exerted to define the goals which are the desired outcome of education. The final objectives should not be just those that are limited or measurable, such as final grades or acceptance to university, but rather those related to a comprehensive vision of each student's future as a mature adult, with all that entails. In the absence of both a departure point for the journey and an endpoint towards which we are striving, it is impossible to plan an effective educational process.

Furthermore, most educational environments are heterogeneous, with needs that vary from child to child. When you couple that with the intensity that characterizes the field of education, it is extremely difficult to produce a unitary method. This leads most of us to rely on our intuition and what we may call "the best interest of the child." Such intuitive education is welcome on the personal-familial level and even, at times, on the communal level; but when managing an educational community with dozens to hundreds of young people, it is very difficult to determine what is truly in the child's best interest. It is not methodical or professional to rely solely on gut feelings, especially when each staff member has his or her own intuition and a differing view of the process.

It is, therefore, necessary to adopt a unifying educational philosophy that will aid in constructing a complete educational-therapeutic process. From within a cohesive philosophy, we can derive all the action to help teens advance from their present situation to one that they truly deserve.

Subcontractors or Educators

The desire to be good to our children often creates a sense of insecurity. We all wonder whether we are good-enough parents or are depriving our children of things essential to their development, not to mention possibly harming them. When our children are young, we tend to blame ourselves for their behavior. As they grow older, we shift the blame onto them. Insecurity, a sense of failure and guilt can provoke frustration and despair as well as a strong desire to learn more. As a result of this desire, professionals began sharing their experiences with others at training sessions and this has led to a range of opportunities to receive parental counseling and guidance.

But our culture's increasing reliance on consultants raises significant questions. Are the vast amount of accumulated knowledge and the many consultants we hire improving our professionalism or perhaps achieving desired results in the short term while damaging the adult-teenager relationship in the long term? Are the consultants making us better parents because of the knowledge we acquire or are we mere 'subcontractors,' implementing methods based on other people's experiences? In other words, who is serving whom: Is the method serving us or are we serving the method?

When a consultant provides us with an air-tight method, they expect us, the educator or parent, to adhere to the prescribed guidelines without expressing our individuality—a wholly unnatural lack of engagement. On the other hand, when a professional provides us with an organized but liberating method—one with built-in flexibility so it can be adapted to our needs—they allow the method to serve us, and we can use it without ceding our natural place. Such a technique may help us improve as educators and as parents.

I came to Yemin Orde after four years spent teaching and educating at Kibbutz Ein Tzurim, working with a wonderful group of young people. That experience left me with a strong appetite to develop further in the field of education. I met Dr. Chaim Peri, the director of Yemin Orde Youth Village, at that juncture in my life. The first meeting was inspiring, exciting and intriguing. He spoke about education as a heavenly pursuit, with many ladders and ropes that link between earth and heaven.

But, when I left his office, I felt confused; I did not know what position I had been offered exactly, and what I was supposed to do with what had been said. Alongside the initial confusion, however, I felt that I had been given the opportunity to join something monumental, a fascinating journey in education. I remember only two things from the meeting: one sentence that he said, and a small, worn leather doll on his desk. The sentence was, "Education leads society and does not lag behind it," and the doll was a leather mouse with large ears and a small mouth, which I interpreted as a message to speak less and listen more.

My first year at Yemin Orde exposed me to an intensive, creative educational enterprise that was fruitful and thought-provoking; from the daily pressures of participating in long staff meetings on educational philosophy and developing programs to following guidelines on how to buy the right type of toilet paper that wouldn't clog the sewage system; from coping with the daily routine to participating in large, meticulously organized Village events. Slowly, I began to understand the way of life at the Village, which was beginning to take shape for me as a holistic, organized educational philosophy.

At the end of that first year, I felt highly fulfilled as a partner in such a meaningful educational framework, but ready to move on from my work at Yemin Orde. I felt that I had become a 'subcontractor' for someone else's educational concept, and that was not what I wanted to do. I went to Chaim and turned in my resignation for the simple reason that even though it was a good approach, I was eager to find my own educational path and not just carry out someone else's theories. Chaim listened attentively and said: "You have seriously misunderstood something."

Chaim then talked about the educational system that would later be called the Village Way. He said that the system was not looking for subcontractors. Instead, it offered an outline in which each educator could find himself and express his own unique talents. The method, he said, which drew upon the wisdom of the founding fathers of the youth village movement in Israel, created a structure in which educators could form their own identity based on professional knowledge and experience while developing their own approaches to education.

This caused me to 're-calculate my route,' to borrow a GPS term. Furthermore, when much later, I was involved in establishing the Village Way Educational Institute, we determined that the guiding principle would be that the Village Way is an educational philosophy designed to help educators formulate their authentic, professional identity. All of this arose out of the belief that education leads society, and that the key to effective education lies in speaking less and listening more.

We Also Have Something to Teach

In his opening speech at the inauguration ceremony for The Hebrew University of Jerusalem on April 1, 1925, famed Israeli poet Haim Nahman Bialik said:

> *"We know well that true wisdom is 'one who learns from all.' The windows of this house will therefore be open on every side, that the fairest fruit produced by man's creative spirit in every land and in every age may enter. But we ourselves are not newcomers to the Kingdom of Spirit, and while learning from all, we also have something to teach."*[3]

One can take Bialik's words far beyond the context in which he describes the place and role of The Hebrew University. We have borrowed his phrasing and adapted them for the role of the educator, and we say in the spirit of his words:

---

3   Ben Yehuda Project, https://benyehuda.org/read/1545

We, the educators, know that true wisdom is one who learns from all, and therefore our school will be open on every side to learn and develop from the fairest fruit of man's creative spirit, from every time and every land. We will be open to research and programs. But let us not forget that we are not newcomers to the Kingdom of Spirit and Deed, and while learning from all, we also have something to teach.

We can all agree on the importance of humility for both parents and educators. We want to learn to do the best by our children and to nurture them. We seek to enrich our toolbox and broaden our thinking, to be worthy of the task of parenting or education. We have much to learn from consultants and facilitators, but we cannot be idle before them, because we also have something to teach. Recognition of our own strengths, experience and understanding are important, and we need to maintain a balance between strength and humility.

Strength is found in our authenticity, the awareness of our power, and our willingness to work toward appropriate responses in real time. Alternatively, it exists in daring to make mistakes and fix them. Humility is found in professionalism, which allows us to learn both from the students and our peers, and as such, acknowledge our weaknesses and act to rectify them. This is also true for the Village Way educational philosophy, which continues to learn from many educators and educational communities in Israel and around the world. Our philosophy is rooted in these main tenets:

- An educator must be authentic and professional.
- Educational communities require a common, unifying educational philosophy.
- An educational philosophy is meant to serve the educator.

As we have learned from all, we wish to say, with strength and humility, that we also have something to teach.

From the Ancient Village
to the Village Way

"I read a book and there was a man
who returned to his village after many years.
I wish I had a village to come back to,
and not just a street with buildings"
        —Lyrics from *I Was Here* by Ivri Lider and Natan Goshen[4]

We're All in This Together: *The Role of Community in Education*

The setting: 1970s—A housing project in Bat Yam, a modest town south of Tel Aviv. In the stairwell of a four-story walkup, a seven-year-old boy wants to try a cigarette he found in the entrance to the building. Who does he need to hide from? His parents? They are at work. His instincts tell him he needs to hide from the entire adult world, so he rushes down the stairs to the basement bomb shelter. Suddenly, a neighbor from the first floor appears, busy locking up her son's bicycle. Seeing the cigarette, she begins to scold him: "What are you doing? Aren't you embarrassed?" If she had been close enough, she might have slapped him across the face.

---

4 *This Love is Ours* [*HaAhava HaZot Shelanu*], (Helicon Music, 2013)

Why did this woman get involved? What was it about that housing project that made the neighbor feel responsible for a boy who was not her son? Was it just that specific woman, or something in the general atmosphere? Perhaps the adult world of housing projects in Israel in the seventies was still grounded in communal experience as opposed to one centered on the individual? How did the boy's parents respond to the fact that an unrelated adult scolded their son? It's likely they took the behavior for granted and would have done the same had they interacted with a neighborhood child. In that housing project, everyone felt a shared sense of duty, hoping that each child would grow to be a person who contributes to their community—a modern urban expression of the African proverb, "It takes a village to raise a child."

If this story took place today—in the same neighborhood or a different one—would a neighbor feel a sense of responsibility for a child that was not her own? And if she felt a sense of responsibility, would she allow herself to criticize someone else's child? How would 21st century Israeli parents, or parents in other parts of the world, feel about this? They would probably consider it inappropriate to intervene in this way. This example illustrates the privatization of communal society, a wider phenomenon that has evolved over the last few centuries. As communities have become less interrelated, the responsibility for a child's education has transitioned from the larger community to the individual.

Yet, in a primal way, we still long for the ancient village. From the dawn of humanity, people have lived in various types of communities, including clans, tribes, villages, migrating communities, and permanent settlements, in which each member felt a sense of commitment to the collective.[5] The ancient villager was surrounded by extended family and acquaintances who helped shape their livelihood, cultural identity and education. The group's values and language were also those of the individual, as were the codes of conduct, the shared history, and the way in which life and the future were understood. The ancient village took

---

5 Yuval Noah Harari, *A Brief History of Humankind* [*Kitsur toldot ha-enoshut*] 2011), 352-378

care of each member's varied needs. Children were educated by parents and grandparents, older siblings, aunts and uncles, as well as other adults. And education was not confined to the classroom. A person's occupation, daily life and rituals combined to form an organic educational experience. From birth, each child was given a roadmap for life. He or she also had a rather clear picture of the future regarding profession, place of residence, the structure of the clan, and their role in the community.

But life has changed drastically in the modern world, particularly in the West. Close-knit communities have slowly disappeared, and responsibilities to the individual have been transferred either to the nuclear family or the public sphere. In some cases, individuals have simply been abandoned with no one held accountable to care for them. With the breakdown of tribal society, the family unit has also shrunk. From an extended family with parental figures involved in raising the young, the bulk of the responsibility for raising children has been left to institutions. The nation-state, with the school system as its representative, has become the central body responsible for formal schooling, while other forms of education are carried out within a series of circles, namely: the family unit, educational institutions, street culture and the peer group. Furthermore, TV, the Internet and social networks have replaced ancient village culture with that of the global village, resulting in adolescents being exposed to countless confusing messages. With no unified goal provided, the external chaos becomes internal and can lead to frustration, even rage. The fact that both parents often work fulltime may mean there is a lack of parental presence in an adolescent's life, as well.

Studies[6] show that a person's basic need for a sense of belonging to a community has not disappeared. In fact, it is more significant than ever. They also suggest that happiness depends on a person's family and communal relationships more than on their financial status or health. This is especially true for children and teenagers. A cohesive educational environment brings emotional stability to a child's internal world, instilling in him or her a sense of belonging and a

---

6   Ibid.

clear picture of the future. Despite the chaos of our technologically advanced world, humankind remains close to the ancient village. Our brains are still wired for the communal structure, even as we live in a world that celebrates individualism. The Village Way is a philosophy that combines the sense of community associated with the ancient village with our contemporary reality.

From Ambuber to Manhattan: *Bringing the Ancient Village to Our Schools*

Recently, I travelled to the United States for the first time in my life to participate in board meetings for ImpactIsrael, the US nonprofit that supports Yemin Orde Youth Village and Village Way Educational Initiatives. I met a committed, values-centered group of people for whom the future of Israeli society matters very much. Just two months prior, I had accompanied some of our graduates on a back-to-roots trip to Ambuber, the Jewish village in the Gondar region of Ethiopia from which their families hailed. The two settings could not have been more different and I couldn't get over the contrast: from the skyscrapers of Manhattan to the *godjo* (mud hut) of the ancient village; from modern urbanites rushing around to villagers conducting their lives at a different pace; from glory and wealth to simplicity and contentment.

The stark differences made me wonder what these two places had in common. On the one hand, we would not want to reconstruct an ancient village in the complex reality of the 21st century. The limited self-realization and hierarchical division of labor wouldn't suit us. But on the other hand, as I met with educational entrepreneurs in Manhattan who shared their challenges helping young people feel a sense of grounding, I realized that we are all humans and feel the need for certain aspects of the ancient village including humility, interdependence, common language and a coherent environment with clear rules and values. We can all learn from the way youth are educated in places like rural Ethiopia.

How can we create a 'village-style' educational community for children and teens that reflects the lessons of living communally? This book is an invitation to embark on a journey toward that destination. Together, we will navigate the labyrinth of adolescence, allowing ourselves to experience moments of confusion and doubt while planning a path that is both spontaneous and structured. Our journey will require that we get familiar with the educational space and all the players within it, including parent, teacher, informal educator and school principal. We will also need to confront our own weaknesses, even though the culture sometimes expects us to be all-knowing leaders.

We developed our philosophy through our experiences with youth from the social and geographic periphery of Israeli society, but this book is not just about at-risk kids. We can use the experiences of our colleagues—educators working with youth at-risk across Israel—to understand young people from other places too. After all, our students are much more than a group with certain perceived characteristics. Here in Israel, our students have been given names such as immigrant youth, at-risk youth, minority youth and marginalized youth, among others. But the names we use to describe them don't really reflect the truth of their lives. Ultimately, they are just young people on a quest to find themselves, like any other adolescent.

There is no such thing as an educational approach aimed only at youth at-risk, but throughout this book, we'll use real life stories from Village Way educational communities to acquaint ourselves with the tools necessary to make growth-oriented educational choices for all kinds of students, according to the Village Way educational philosophy.

Three Foundational Principles of the Village Way

1. It takes a village to raise a child.
2. Every child needs a **supportive adult**[7] who believes in him or her.
3. A young person is an individual in search for meaning.

---

7   In this book, the term "supportive adult" is used to refer to any adult who serves a meaningful role in the life of a teenager, ideally someone who is authentic, empathetic, caring, stable and consistent. Such an individual sets boundaries and standards, and often remains a significant presence in the young person's life long after s/he is no longer physically present in a young person's life.

Sitting in a training session in an air-conditioned room, we could easily commit to these three principles. But let's face it—sometimes we respond to situations in ways that don't align with our beliefs. When dealing with a group of violent teenagers, it can be difficult to see them as good people yearning for meaning. It is also hard to act like a supportive adult when you feel humiliated in front of angry teenagers. That's a feeling I know well!

Lights-Out at the Youth Village: *A Formative Experience*

It was just before lights-out for the young people who lived and studied at Yemin Orde Youth Village, where I led our informal education program. I got a call from my wife: "When will you be home?" I told her the evening was shaping up to be a calm one, and I would soon be leaving the Village for home. I was really looking forward to going home as the day had been a draining one, but suddenly, I got another phone call, this time from Hagit, an informal educator[8] for the ninth-grade girls. "There is a big party here at the clubhouse. We're trying to stop it, but they're just completely ignoring us," she said, referring to the group of teens under her supervision. "Who's we? And what is so complicated?" I asked. The only response I received was "Please come."

So, instead of heading home to my own family, I went to the clubhouse, a room designated for the kids to relax during free hours. The informal educators were standing around while the kids were having a good time with loud music and dancing. Experience had taught us that after these parties, the teens had a hard time regulating the level of adrenaline in their bodies and would often go looking for additional excitement through alcohol or other illegal activities. We knew if we did not control the party now, the night could progress in an unsafe direction.

---

8   The informal educator works closely with the teenagers in the afterschool hours, and helps them meet a variety of needs.

I went into the clubhouse, walking between dancing boys and girls, and pushed my way to the improvised DJ stand. I pulled the cord from the electrical outlet, picked up the whole sound system and was about to leave the clubhouse. The sudden silence was very tense. The dancers surrounded me in anger and shouted "Why? What's the problem with us having fun?" This soon progressed towards violence, at first cursing and then a group attempt to forcefully remove the speakers from my hands. Angry and hurt, I did not let go. I raised my voice and managed to extricate myself. Just before I left the clubhouse, Iris, a ninth-grade student, approached me with tears in her eyes, shouting: "You're always sure that you're right but you're just a son-of-a-bitch who doesn't understand anything!"

Despite the hubbub, we managed to stop the party so that lights-out could carry on as expected. The staff members who did not witness what I had experienced inside the clubhouse were standing outside looking satisfied. But on the way to the office carrying the speakers, I felt humiliated at finding myself surrounded by kids, for whom I cared very much, shoving me and cursing. Those who were less violent but blocked my way disappointed me just as much. I was angry at the angry kids, at disrespectful Iris, and I was searching for a target to blame. For a moment, I blamed myself and then I immediately became defensive and blamed the informal educator, the staff, and then came back to myself. Confused, I called a senior Village staff member and asked him to take over managing the crisis—I just couldn't go on. I began to realize that my immediate response had been one-sided, perhaps even aggressive. I had been looking for a quick fix, and that had resulted in an aggressive response from the kids.

I never imagined they would dare to react that way. I had just been on autopilot after a busy day. I had taken a step that was supposed to lead to a certain result, but I had not adequately evaluated the potential consequences. The senior staff member arrived, all relaxed. I filled him in on the details and transferred the responsibility over to him. He said he would calm things down, but we would continue dealing with the matter together the next day.

But before the staff could confront the issue together, Iris, who had been so angry, came to speak to me. I was not in the right mindset to deal with her, but she didn't wait for me to be ready. Standing in my way, she apologized for what she had said and added that she knew her behavior was not okay, but because she felt hurt, it had just come out. I responded: "I won't lie. I was hurt, and I'm finding it hard to forgive you right now. And what you did, mostly did harm to you."

This encounter with her happened too soon after the event for me to respond in a balanced way. On the way home that day, I wondered: Why didn't I accept her apology? Why didn't I appreciate the step she took? I guess I just could not at that point. But soon, I had another opportunity.

I arrived at the office the next morning and found Iris and her older brother, Yaniv, waiting for me. Iris apologized again, and this time I accepted her apology before she returned to class. I then turned to Yaniv, a high school senior who had been at the party with his friends, and asked him "What happened? How did we come to this?" Yaniv had been my student and we had a close relationship. He was happy to tell me his side of the story: "My sister arrived at the Village this year, and you know, she has a physical disability which really affects her self-esteem, so she hasn't really managed to fit into her group socially. Yesterday was her birthday, and my friends helped me throw a party for her. Her friends got excited, and that was important to me. I wanted to make her happy."

Suddenly, the sentence Iris had angrily shouted that night reverberated in my head: "You think you are always right." Those words suddenly sounded different. I asked Yaniv why he hadn't asked permission to have the party. He answered: "I wasn't planning on it being a big party, so I didn't think I needed to, and anyway, would you have approved a dance party that included senior boys partying with ninth-grade girls?" I could see his point. During the stand-off with the angry kids, the situation had been bleak; but now, the full picture began to come into focus. The reality was much more complex than it had appeared just before lights-out.

Only the Strong Survive: *Challenges Make us Better Educators*

We know that human beings seek meaning, and that includes teens. Yet, how difficult it is for us to identify this longing in real time! Yaniv did what he did for his sister out of a sense of love for her, while I saw only an unauthorized party. The party did indeed have to be stopped and, perhaps, there was no choice but to stop it in a one-sided way; but we skipped some important steps. We all pay a heavy price for looking for a quick fix. If I had been in a more open mindset, I could have asked: What's the reason for this party? Why is it important to those who organized it? What are the consequences of a one-sided response? What does it convey to the kids? I could have recalled that my authority did not stem from physical strength. After all, the teens are stronger than we are. Therefore, we need to avoid playing in the physical arena as much as possible. I learned that day that what we think are the most stressful days and worst timing may actually open the door for the most learning. To thrive in education, we need to see the broader picture and seek help from colleagues who can provide backup while keeping us in the loop. We need to explore specific events, analyze them, and learn for the next time.

It's this kind of investigation that has led to the three foundational principles of the Village Way educational philosophy.

1. **It takes a village to raise a child. Every educational community requires common values and a commitment to collective responsibility.**
Forming an educational community increases the impact of our efforts to educate young people so that the whole will be greater than the sum of its parts. This connection can be made through defining **communal values,**

developing a **common language,** and accepting **collective educational responsibility**.

Communal Values

As previously stated, the ancient village had clear rules that expressed the collective values and helped the adolescent to understand what was expected. Our current era is characterized by such an abundance of contradictory messages that young people frequently do not know what is allowed or expected of them. Likewise, each educator tends to emphasize values that reflect their personal outlook. That is why it is important that every educational community establish communal values while also allowing plenty of room for disagreement.

Common Language

For every endeavor, a language develops that reflects its values. A common language does not mean that all adults recite from the same playbook provided by a consultant. It means that the messages are clear, the language is shared, and every person expresses the message in his or her own way. Language has the power to shape reality, not only describe it. Common language emerges organically, and slang plays an important role in the formation of a local language. But in the absence of a common parlance, street language may fill the void, with adults using disrespectful language when trying to communicate with youth. It is therefore important that we develop a common language.

Collective Responsibility

With common values and language in place, every adult in an educational community has educational responsibility for the children. Each one has their own job description and unique mission—teacher, secretary, food service, maintenance professional, therapist, and others. Yet, in the Village Way, there is also an expectation that every adult assumes general responsibility for all children. This is expressed by saying hello to each child, by positively recognizing every kid that does a good deed, and by openly talking with every young person who is behaving inappropriately.

Sometimes, we see a kid who is doing something forbidden and we debate whether to respond. Educational responsibility means choosing to respond because an adult who ignores a child is sending a message. That message could be that the child's actions are technically forbidden but are de facto permitted, or that the action is indeed forbidden but the adult just doesn't care about the child. The third possible message is: "I am afraid to reprimand you." Many of us have heard teenagers say of an educator: "He didn't dare say something to me!" Teens needs to know that we care about them and that we are *not* afraid of them. Remember the neighbor from the first floor in Bat Yam who reprimanded the smoking child? She was acting with educational responsibility towards a child who was not technically hers but was a part of her community.

2.   Every child needs a supportive adult who will believe in him or her. There was a modern Chassidic rabbi who often said: "All a child needs is at least one adult who believes in him." With due respect to the Rabbi, I believe a child needs significantly more than that, but I agree with the intention of the statement: A child needs support to build emotional resilience. Within the proverbial village, reliable adults are needed to believe in the child and to help him feel secure enough to make mistakes.

Adolescence is like a raging river that we must cross. To do so, a teenager looks for something to hold on to. Before grabbing a tree or rock, he or she may shake it to make sure it is stable. If it is, the teenager will hold on with confidence. We, the supportive adults in the village, need to understand that being an adult means withstanding this shaking test of adolescence. Ironically, it is crucial that adults be so strong that young people will feel like rebelling against them. Rebellion is an important part of development, and we adults need to be entities worthy of their rebellion.

3.   Children and teens search for meaning in life, just as adults do.

In *Man's Search for Meaning*, psychologist Victor Frankl teaches that a wish for meaning is an integral aspect of all human beings.[9] This concept can be seen clearly in educational situations. Even if it seems that a child's only wish in life is to disrupt the routine, these are expressions of a deep longing for meaning, a wish to be good and do good. Through their behavior, the child is shouting "Help me!" It is our job as supportive adults to let our youth know that we approve of their internal longing and that we will help them pursue their own sense of inner meaning.

The Village Way Roadmap: *A Journey through Four Stations*

A journey through the Village Way is a journey through four stations; each clarifies an essential element of the Village Way roadmap. As we move through each station, which corresponds to each chapter in this book, we will identify potential challenges and possible courses of action. In the final chapter, we will review the roadmap and put the methodology into practice by tackling the issue of cultural diversity within education.

As you can see in the graphic depiction on the following page, the Village Way roadmap is comprised of two axes, two circles, and four corners of the educational field. The first chapter of this book will look at real-life stories related to the perception of time and its role in education and how time can be used as a touchstone, an 'anchor,' through which to form a personal identity.

The second chapter deals with situations related to values and ethics, known in Jewish tradition as *derech eretz*. In this chapter, we will delve into the importance of physical space and structures, and how they can influence a person's emotional and psychological resilience.

The third chapter connects the emphasis on time and space to what is known in Jewish mysticism as *tikkun*, or repair. Depicted in the illustration as 'circles of repair,' this concept is presented through stories of individual

---

9   Viktor E. Frankl, *Man's Search for Meaning: An Introduction to Logotherapy* (New York: Simon & Schuster,1984)

growth in *Tikkun HaLev*, self-improvement, and *Tikkun Olam*, improving society as a whole.

The fourth chapter describes the limits of the educational field in which we function—the difficulties and opportunities that exist within those limits and how to grow from within them.

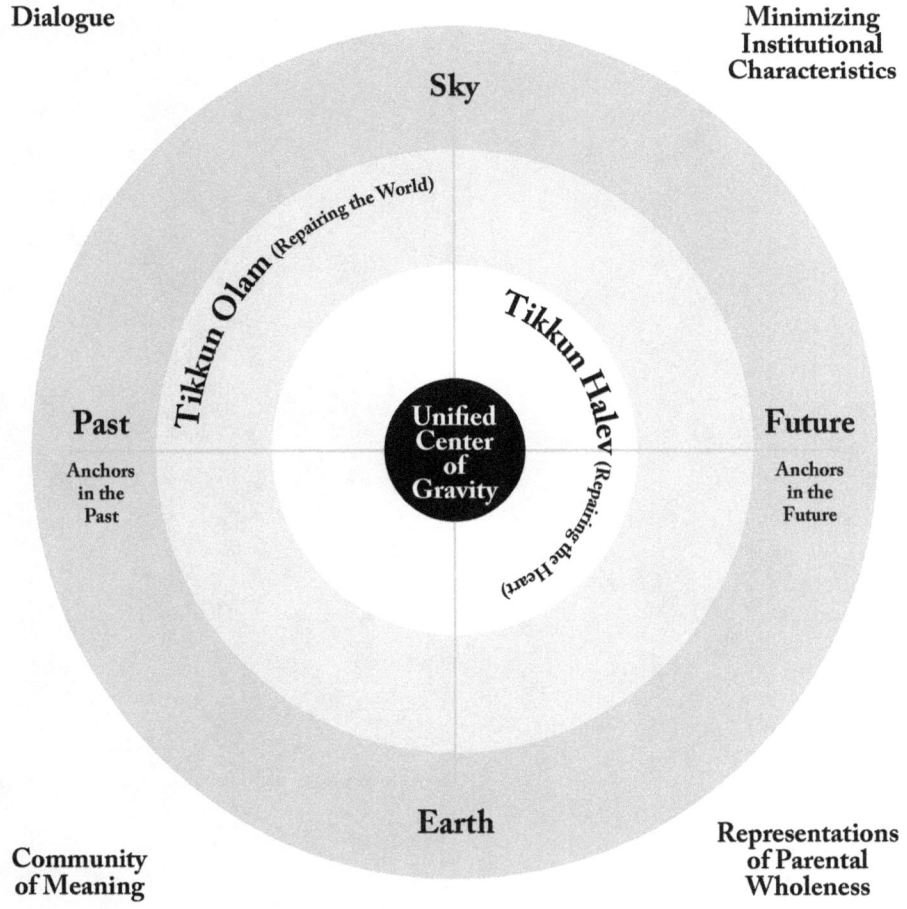

CHAPTER 1

Time as an Anchor for Identity: *Anchors in the Past and the Future*

"And of course, there was the Hebrew teacher. He had us write an essay on "What I want to be when I grow up." I sat, and thought, and got upset. I didn't know what to write. Then I wrote and I wrote as if in a trance. I want to have roots and wings, I wrote. Why should one give up on the roots if one's heart desires wings? (I wrote three question marks, and then I erased two.) The roots miss out on so much when they are stuck deep in the ground and cannot fly or see the tremendous tops of the trees and the great forest. The birds on the tree, who are lucky to have wings, are missing the grip on the ground, and their nests depend on the mercy of the storm winds and the sturdiness of the tree, under whose branches they take shelter. Therefore, I concluded: When I grow up, I want to be a man with roots and wings."[10]

—Amnon Shamosh, Israeli writer

Hakuna Matata: *Either Run or Learn*

In the Disney movie, *The Lion King*[11], a lion cub named Simba runs away from his home in Pride Rock because he feels responsible for his father's death. Lonely and in pain, Simba wanders until he meets Timon and Pumba, a meerkat and a wild boar whose life philosophy is *"hakuna*

---

10 Amnon Shamosh. *"Tmunot MeBeit Hasefer Ha'amami," in Kane Ve-Kinamon [Calamus and Cinnamon]*, (Massada, 1979)

11 *The Lion King*, dirs. Roger Allers and Rob Minkoff (1994: Disney)

matata," which means "Don't worry, put your past behind you." We then watch as Simba grows from a lion cub into an adolescent, fitting in well in the jungle, until his childhood friend Nala arrives, asking that he return to Pride Rock to help. Simba hesitates somewhat, but following his 'live in the now' philosophy, refuses.

At the climax of the film, a monkey called Rafiki meets Simba and asks: "Who are you?" Simba says that he once knew who he was, but no longer does. Rafiki then reminds Simba of his father and his past and makes him realize he must return home. But a gap remains between knowing the right course of action and the ability to implement it. Simba understands this situation and replies: "But going back means I'll have to face my past. And I've been running from it for so long."

At this point, Rafiki hits Simba over the head. "Ow!" Simba cries in pain. "What was that for?" Rafiki replies with a grin: "It doesn't matter! It's in the past!" Simba then says: "But it still hurt." Rafiki answers wisely "Then the past *can* hurt. But the way I see it, you can either run from it or learn from it."

Simba is a wonderful representation of teens who feel unsuccessful or believe they are disappointing the adults in their lives. They adapt themselves to the Hakuna Matata, 'live in the now,' mentality in order to survive. The way to help them is to assume the role of Rafiki, to remind them of who they are through a powerful experience from their past, and in this way, to make them feel needed. They, like Simba, are searching for meaning.

"Know from Where You Come:" *Having A Relationship with the Past*

> *I'm returning to the past to gather fireflies*
> *To build with them a ladder of stars*
> *Pathways I didn't take, which could not have been there*
> *Maybe they are still waiting there for me.*
> *If you will go there, my heart*

Come to the past without stopping
We will gather all the good
We will gather all the innocence
We will gather fireflies and return... I go back to the past, with no
fear of the time
I can tell right from wrong[12]
       —From *Fireflies* by Esther Shamir, Israeli singer and naturopath

The past never disappears. It is crucial to address its role in forming our identity. Are we able to see the points of light even in the most complex past? Can we—as in the wonderful poem by Esther Shamir—travel with the young people in our lives into their pasts to collect fireflies and build a ladder of stars? Can we go fearlessly into the past, learning to distinguish the good from the bad, and collecting the good before returning?

Our experience and perception of the future influence how each of us behaves in the present, whether we are conscious of this or not. Boys and girls reach adolescence with a range of experiences, perceptions and beliefs about their abilities, about what lies ahead in their future, and about society around them. Still, most of their efforts, and our work with them, relate to the here and now. They are busy testing their own limits and those of the world around them, while forming a personal, social, sexual and cultural identity. Our ongoing role is supporting them in this mission.

When we try to explain to teens the consequences of their actions and decisions, we often get a response indicating, verbally or otherwise, "I don't care," or "I like it like this." This stems from the natural teenage tendency to live in the moment. Lurking behind that response is often a whole array of beliefs about their capabilities and what awaits them in the future. When we add to adolescence past experiences of difficulty, disappointment, or crisis, and when successes are few and not adequately recognized by the adults in their world, then positive experiences seem

---

12   Esther Shamir." Fireflies [*Gachliyot*]," *Because of the People I Like* (2003), translated by Ayelet Bukai, in hebrewsongs.com.

totally out of reach. When the adults in their lives, their natural role models, struggle to get ahead despite putting in hard work, or alternatively, when they have given up their struggle and give in to the harsh reality of their lives, then the young person often retreats further into the feeling of living just for the moment. When someone has no past successes to recall and no hope for a better future, the result is thoughtless behavior with immediate benefits—just like Simba in the early part of *The Lion King*. Everyone creates their own narrative based on their understanding of what their struggles and their successes (if any) say about them. Understanding our own narrative is often the key to change and growth.

Exposing Roots

Staying in contact with former students at different points in their lives allows us to witness the wonders of self-development and to get a closer look at what we refer to as the **past-future timeline**.

I met up with Hagit when I was visiting her as her family sat shiva, after her father died. While cradling her baby, she told me how our shared analysis of her narrative, including identifying 'anchors' or key moments in her past, had helped her during her high school years and continues to guide her today.

Hagit explains:

> *My mother died when I was a very young girl before we arrived in Israel from Ethiopia. For as long as I can remember, I have had a foggy memory of her, of a song she would sing and the feeling of her being physically near me—the smell, the warmth, and the security. This memory was not the kind you cuddle up with, but the kind that always reminds you of what is missing. The memory was more of a continuous longing. My father remarried when I was young, and when we got to Israel, my stepmother was registered as my mother, and that is how she was known at my school. For years, I was disoriented, unsure of my place at home. I did not know if my*

stepmother really accepted us. She often gave me the sense that I did not belong in the family, a feeling that hurt me deeply. I had strong feelings of longing, guilt and frustration. Every attempt to recall the past and describe it was extremely difficult for me.

I remember in seventh grade, when we had to do a big family history project, I didn't know what to do. All my classmates were so happy with their projects. They put in a lot of work, bringing in pictures of their extended families and of themselves as babies. I did not even have pictures from the village where I was born. All the pictures of my childhood were locked in my memory. I avoided it. I never revealed to my classmates that the woman known as my mother was my stepmother and that I had a previous family history. Until that point, I had been a rather good student, but I started to deal with the pain that this project stirred up by ditching school, disappearing, drinking and smoking. I felt terrible that I was neglecting my studies, but I didn't want the other kids in my class to ask questions and dig up the past. I knew that I didn't want to expose the fact that the woman known as my mother was my stepmother.

Then in eleventh grade, I had a conversation with you, Dotan, and somehow, I shared with you that my mother had died. Finally, I had put down the heavy load I had been carrying all those years, and together, we aired it out and looked at it from different angles. I told you about the difficult feelings, the pain and anger. I learned to see how I could live with the scars and how to appreciate my own abilities. I remember that you told me: "Your mother is such a meaningful presence in your life, and I know that she will continue to serve an important role in your life in the years to come." I discovered that I had a lot of strength because of what happened in the past. I also felt empowered because of my decision to be a different kind of parent than my stepmother, a more loving one. Since I have become a mother, I really feel how much that conversation impacts so many of my choices.

The meeting with Hagit moved me very much. The timeline of her life, the way in which she understands and lives it, steadies her, and gives her direction. The **anchors in her past** are true touchstones that she can lean on and from which she can derive the strength to continue.

From this past, Hagit imagines a picture of the future toward which she is progressing. Rather than a mere sequence of incidents, life is a series of stories. As educators, we can help tell the story and generate a lesson from each event, which we can then share with the young person and the supportive adults in their lives.

This may be familiar to many educators as the narrative approach, a therapeutic method that helps individuals find meaning in life through organizing life events in a continuous chronological order, allowing each person to piece together a coherent description of himself. A successful narrative process provides people with a sense of continuity and meaning in their lives and serves as a foundation for organizing their daily life and interpreting the experiences to come. According to the narrative approach, shaping our lives relies, not just on understanding the past, but rather on structuring the future utilizing life narratives together with the tools of emotional resilience, imagination and creativity. A person can make a difference in his own life if he changes the way he constructs and tells the story of his life to himself and others. The change requires one to stop focusing on problems, and instead, highlight strengths.

The narrative concept as applied to education connects the present reality with a constructive understanding of the person's personal story. Clarifying a teenager's past strengths directly impacts their present. They begin to perceive themselves and their surroundings in a more positive, empowered light. In the educational process, we seek to relate to this narrative and to create, for the youth and for ourselves, 'anchors in the past' and **anchors in the future**; these provide stability and enable us to investigate the past, even if it is a complex one, and to find faith in a better future.

What's Your Story, Kid?

It is important to create opportunities in which we ask teenagers to tell their story. It is best to begin by doing this individually, in private conversations or in essay projects. Then at a more advanced stage, we can progress to making space for telling the story in a group framework during social activities, homeroom, or group therapy, or around the holiday or dinner table with family. Part of our job as educators is to offer alternative perspectives on a familiar story. In one educator training session, we asked the staff members to write down facts related to the child's past and weave together two stories: the story the child is currently telling themselves, and the story that we want them to be telling themselves in order for them to progress toward a better future. This is the result:

The teen says:

> *For as long as I can remember, I have basically raised myself. I was what people call a 'latchkey kid,' but in my case, it was also 'lunch-alone kid,' and 'homework-alone kid,' and 'public-park kid' and 'dinner-alone kid,' and sometimes even 'tells-his-own-bedtime-story kid.' My parents would both leave early for work, sometimes before I woke up, leaving me a sandwich for school on the kitchen table. They would come back late in the evening without any energy to deal with me or my siblings.*

We hope to teach the teen to narrate it like this:

> *I grew up in a house where there was much value placed on a strong work ethic. Even though my parents were not well-educated, it was really important to them that their children study and succeed in life. Therefore, they worked very hard, from morning until night, so that we wouldn't have to go without and to help us fund our higher education.*

The teen says:

> *You know the feeling that no one really wants you or cares about you? I do because that is exactly what I was, a lost kid whose parents and family just didn't want him around because he took time away from their lives. By seventh grade, my parents had shipped me off to a youth village. I remember the day I first arrived; my dad put down the bags in my new room with empty walls and said, "You see? It's not that bad." And then he left, leaving me with adults and kids I didn't know and with a big hole in my soul.*

We want to encourage him to say:

> *If there is one thing that I thank my parents for, it is having the courage to send me to a youth village. I grew up in a tough neighborhood, and my chances of getting ahead had I stayed were nearly zero. I remember the day that my dad took me to the boarding school for the first time. I can only imagine how hard it was for him, how he had to hide his tears and rush to leave. Thanks to the great sacrifice that he and my mother made, I am the person I am today, and for that I sincerely thank them.*

The teen says:

> *In our house, we spoke only Russian—Russian, Russian, Russian all the time! My parents, who emigrated from Belarus, didn't try very hard to learn Hebrew and spoke to us only in their native language. While all my friends were already speaking, laughing, and even cursing in Hebrew, my siblings and I were forced to memorize poems by Pushkin. It was most embarrassing around my Israeli friends, so I didn't invite them over.*

We want to help them see it like this:

In our house, we spoke only Russian. My parents, who emigrated from Belarus, thought it would be a good idea to speak to us only in their native language, and in doing so, provide us with another language. How right they were! Today, even my children understand the language and can communicate with their grandparents.

The teen says:

From a young age, I had to work during every school vacation to help my family. While other kids were resting, at camp or enjoying doing nothing, I busted my ass in the summer heat just to add a few measly shekels to the family's budget. I would leave early in the morning with my dad and wait at the bus stop on the way to the factory, praying that none of my friends would pass by and see me.

We want to suggest another narrative:

From a young age, I worked during every school vacation to help my family. That time in my life taught me to be independent and responsible, and helped me to understand what is truly important. I worked hard, sure, but I also learned how important it is to take advantage of every moment. When other kids were dealing with all kinds of childish things, I was already earning my first paycheck.

Deception or Perception

Choosing to weave together a story from past strengths can feel incomplete and maybe even a bit false. After all, one would think that a child knows very well whether he came to live at a youth village because his parents neglected him, or because his parents wanted him to build a brighter future and knew that they had limited resources at home. And yet, this is not so, as so often children do not always see the bigger picture. We have found that kids often feel unwanted because that is the story that they tell themselves. Only after they have grown up and gone through a reframing of their pasts, can they understand the complex situations that parents face. The art of education does not seek to ignore a complex reality, but rather to posit an additional possible truth, even when facts may indicate the opposite.

We as educators can easily see such teenagers as disadvantaged, but our role is to uncover additional layers. In creating this change, we allow the children to expand their limited perspective and tell their true story in a way that promotes a broader perspective.

The Past and the Future in the Educational Process

An educator who works with the timeline is consciously addressing the power accessible to us all through illuminating 'anchors in the past' and forming 'anchors in the future.' As a first step, it is important that we learn to see our students and ourselves as complex and multidimensional, including the past as we have truly experienced it. This observation will accompany us through various kinds of lessons. Over time, we will learn to identify the places where our students' behaviors may present an opportunity to delve into 'anchors' in the past or future.

This is how it was with Hagit, the student who talked about the roots project in which she only mentioned her stepmother. As she recalled our conversation, I too remembered her story and the event that became a turning point in our dialogue and educational process. Hagit did not mention—and probably didn't remember –how we came to discuss her 'anchors in the past,' or how she sees herself in the future. For me, however, as her educator and homeroom teacher, it was an unforgettable and influential educational moment:

> It was during a grade-wide activity during the Hebrew month of
> Elul, a time for personal reflection, entitled "A journey to myself and
> to my people." As a part of the activity, the kids moved between four
> stations, each with an experiential activity related to significant

figures from their personal past or the shared national past. Hagit
moved between the stations and strongly objected to participating in
an activity where the kids had to "explore their past." At one point,
she also interfered with everyone else's experience. It would have
been easy to interpret her behavior as rude since she simply mocked
everyone around her. I took advantage of the transition time between
stations to take her aside and ask her quietly, without accusation:
"What are you trying to tell us?" I thought her opposition came from
something deeper than her declaration of "I don't feel like it." It was
a simple question that led to an answer that had been begging to get
out into the open for a very long time. At one of the stations, the kids
were asked to think of a person who was dear to them and was no
longer living, to light a candle for that person and decide on a good
deed they would do in their honor. That station, my question, and
perhaps the right timing, caused Hagit to tell me about the death of
her mother at a young age and about her stepmother.

This story was a milestone in my educational journey, one I often
remember when facing children and adolescents who are actively or
passively opposing an activity. What was it about dealing with the past
as part of a roots project in seventh grade that led Hagit to reclusion,
smoking and apathy, and what was it about the process in eleventh grade
that enabled her to share this story and grow in a positive direction?

The answer to this question is comprised of factors partly dependent
on the student, such as age, maturity and stage in life. It is also dependent
on us as educators, the simple presence of a supportive adult and an
assignment that invites introspective observation of the past, rather than
one that is part of the required curriculum. The outcome seems to have
also been helped by good timing and by my decision to delay my response
to her initial resistance, which I could have just interpreted as disrespect.
Success is determined by our ability to consider what resistance is really

trying to impart. We must be ready to collect data from below the surface, which we can understand with our educational instincts.

Hagit's story is an example of how you develop **personal and cultural anchors** in the past.

1. In the first stage, we allow for **an introduction to the past**, placing it in the legitimate space of the educational environment. We start by sharing from our own life stories as we give assignments related to the students' personal and cultural pasts. These assignments should spark positive memories, like fireflies flickering through the past.

2. In the second stage, we deal with **understanding the personal narrative**. After the initial connection to memories and experiences, we observe the past as a narrative, in a way that creates distance between the young person and the experience they went through. For the first time, we look at the past from the outside, at a distance.

3. The third stage consists of identifying **anchors in the past,** marking key momentous events that we can rely on in the present and that will serve as building blocks for the future. This is achieved by offering alternative perspectives and then identifying successes, allowing the young person to draft a detailed plan for the future.

What to Do When the Past Drags You Down

The weight of the past is a force in our lives, and like any other force, it may work *for us* or *against us*. Clearly, if we want to have an impact on a person's future, we need to consider his past. But what do we do when the past is extremely difficult? In such cases, is it beneficial for us to relate to and be reminded of the past? The writer Aharon Appelfeld writes in his book *The Story of Life*: "The past, even the most difficult, is not a defect or a shame, but a living thing."[13] Our past is our quarry to be excavated;

---

13 Aharon Appelfeld, *The Story of Life* (New York: Schocken Press, 2006)

it is part of who we are and carries inherently formative power. When we consider the element of time in a person's life and identity, we see it as a source of security, power and influence that holds the ship steady, despite occasionally getting stuck.

In every past, even the most difficult, it is possible to find sources of strength and light. Education that provides a conscious place for this force can then channel it toward development. The word for crisis in modern Hebrew is *mashber*. In ancient Hebrew, *mashber* was a stool on which a woman sat during childbirth, at a time in history when giving birth was a life-threatening process. From this word arose the cliché in Hebrew that in every crisis there is an opportunity for new birth. However true this may be, it is important to remember that growth does not always appear immediately after a crisis. The period between the crisis and the growth is also vital to the process.

When I was giving a lecture at Oranim Academic College on 'anchors in the past,' there was a college student who became angry: "I lost my older brother, and every time someone talks to me about the past, that is the first experience that comes to mind. It has ripped my family apart, and there is no silver lining. Any attempt to find a positive spin on this story is such a phony delusion."

My response to this expression is simple: We have no intention of covering up the pain. We are committed to understanding the brokenness and pain long before we celebrate the crisis as potential for growth.

The question then arises—how can I, as an educator, deal with these sensitive subjects? This isn't my field, after all. There are professionals who have been trained for it, such as guidance counselors or therapists. How can I ignore the multiple dimensions of a child during the educational process? The answer is—we cannot ignore a child's emotional needs during this process. It is important to work cautiously and sensitively, to sharpen our senses and discuss the issue. This is not an easy process. Just like in a militarized zone, when a soldier notices a landmine, he is required to mark the area and call in a specialized unit. He does not ignore the mine, but he also does not try to handle it by himself. He shows responsibility, acknowledges his limitations, and calls in those trained to take care of it.

There is a justifiable concern that educators, in the absence of the right professional training and tools, might try to treat students with traumatic pasts, although they are not properly qualified to do so. In many schools, there is no professional training for personal conversations with students. Educators are required to pass a CPR and First Aid course, but are not always required to learn about the signs of emotional crisis in children or to provide emotional first aid. There is a delicate balance between educator and therapist—an educator is not and should not be a therapist. However, in a successful educational process, there ought to be a meaningful relationship between educator and student, so that sensitive conversations are possible. Getting training in the areas in which we are lacking, both as individual educators and as a team, can only benefit all parties involved.

As educators, we move along the 'timeline' with our students; neither erasing the past, nor embellishing it. Instead, we look at various ways to narrate it. We approach the difficult experiences like an open wound, which requires that we identify the damage and begin the healing process. Only then, can we learn to live with the scars and find the power with which to progress.

No one can bring Hagit's dead mother back, nor do we discount Hagit's painful experience of being orphaned so early in life. But we can help her to recount positive early memories of her mother, and to observe her early life experience from a distance, so that she can see that the totality of her experiences helped her become sensitive, independent and caring. We can then help her imagine how the home and family she will want to establish might look, using her own diverse life experiences as a guide.

Anchors in the Future

If You Don't Eat, You Won't Grow

"What will become of you?"

That is a sentence often used by parents and educators after a teenager engages in troublesome behavior. Meaning, if you keep acting like this, where is it going to get you? You are on the fast track to nowhere. How many of us have heard or said the sentence: "If you don't eat, you won't grow," or the educational version: "If you don't study, you won't succeed," or: "There is no way you're going to pass your finals if you go out with your friends tonight." I can still hear the words spoken by a boy at Ofek Juvenile Prison to a parole officer. The boy said to him, "The first time I heard a parole officer say to me 'If you don't cooperate you will end up in Ofek Prison,' I was 10 years old. I knew then that I would end up in juvenile prison."

That boy was shouting something at the top of his lungs that we all need to hear. There are many things we can learn from him and other young people including:

- **Do not threaten:** A threat is familiar language for teenagers, especially for those children labeled as "criminals."
- **Do not create a negative picture of the future:** More than frightening the teen, a threat creates a negative image of his future. And in the absence of a more positive potential image, the child's future aligns itself with what is offered.
- **Do not impose conditions on the future:** The future will come whether we want it to or not. The question is how we will influence it.

You're Going to Grow, So Let's Eat

Let's return to the discussion of common expressions in our language. It's not for nothing that a teenager's common answer when an adult asks him: "What will become of you?" ranges from "Everything will be fine" to "I can't predict the future" to "What do I care?" It is obvious to the teenager that the question itself anticipates a negative future.

Instead of saying: "If you don't eat, you won't grow," I hope to raise my own kids with the sentence: "You are going to grow up, so let's sit and eat." Seemingly straightforward, the sentiment is not simplistic. It suggests that the future is here, and it is positive. It shines down on our actions in the present.

If we take this sentence and apply it to any interaction, we will find that it changes the style of the conversation, from **antagonistic** to **cooperative.** The sentence: "We are going to pass the final exams, so today there is a special study session and everyone will be attending," sounds much better than the sentence: "I already passed my final exams while you haven't, so whoever doesn't come to the study session better not complain to me afterwards about your grade, and don't be surprised if you fail." The sentence: "You are going to be officers in the army, so get used to being on time," will foster more cooperation than the sentiment: "How will you ever make it in the army? You guys are spoiled and undisciplined."

Having said that, let's also recognize the instances in which parents and educators have used threats which seemingly proved successful. After all, many of us were raised with the threat method, and we think of ourselves as at least relatively successful! During moments of crisis, our default is to go back to what we are used to and what we ourselves absorbed, and without being aware of it, we imitate both the positive aspects of our upbringing along with the mistakes.

So, there may indeed be something positive in a threat that achieves immediate results expressed by a temporary calm, but we must honestly ask two questions: Is the threatening style appropriate for kids growing up in the reality of the 21st century? And does the threat have a long-term effect?

A threat may be seen by teenagers as an invitation to a battle of wills and may push them unconsciously towards a prohibited action. In some cases, they may not feel fear, but opposition, in response to a threat. In others, the threat may work in the short term, but in the long term, it may contribute to the formation of submissive, hesitant and even fearful young men and women. We want to educate teenagers to break through the glass ceiling. A person driven by threats will not dare to try or make mistakes. To achieve success, it is crucial to have the inner conviction to experiment, and never give in to false prophets and convention.

First Make it There, Then We'll Talk

Sometimes provocation by adults is seen as incentive by teenagers to prove themselves. In such cases, a teenager has generally experienced success in the past, which serves as an additional source of strength. That strength enables them to prove to the adult questioning them that they can succeed again. To those who have not experienced success and have no sources of strength, it can be painful and destructive. Let's not gamble on which one it will be.

> *One afternoon, we played basketball—four staff members and two 11th graders. The game became competitive, and this was beginning to overshadow the fun of the game. After I made an unsuccessful play, a student named Abraham said: "You're such a loser." I gave him a look that said "I know we're playing, but cool it." We continued to play, talk, and challenge one another. Abraham taunted me again: "It's because you're a teacher, you guys are all so weak," and laughed. My injured male ego, combined with pride in my profession, produced the question: "Why, what do you want to be?" Abraham answered proudly: "A lawyer." I looked at him and said: "First make it there, then we'll talk."*
>
> *Ten years after that seemingly insignificant event, which I doubt I would have remembered otherwise, Abraham came to visit the*

school and came looking for me. We met briefly, and he said: "First make it there, then we'll talk'—I remember that sentence well. So here I am, about to complete my law degree. The sentence that you said to me back then shook my confidence. I managed to make it, but don't say that to other students—because some of them will hear that sort of comment and quit before even trying." I humbly accepted his message. Abraham was right. I said what I did without thinking, but as educators, we must realize that these kind of doubting messages are too dangerous for our kids.

Teenagers often convey confidence, which allows them to respond to adults with indifference, or even arrogance. Such behavior can trigger aggressive behavior in adults. Soon, we find ourselves dragged into verbal conflicts and threats that border on violence. Our natural tendency is to look at reality in a linear fashion and to make the future conditional upon the present, but the truth is that our perception of ourselves in the future has a significant impact on our behavior in the present. I'd even say that the future affects the present much more than the present affects the future. Every conscious action in the present stems from the future result that we seek to achieve. Knowing what we want will instantly affect our present actions.

Draw Me a Future

The natural human fear of the unknown is shared among all people. There are those whom it fills with positive bursts of adrenaline born of curiosity, and those who are paralyzed by it. 'Anchors in the future' connect with one another to create a horizon of expectations, ambitions and hopes that pave the way for progress. At the Village Way, we call this an **image of the future**. To help teenagers develop one, we introduce them to potential positive pictures of their future. It is our job as educators to believe in every teenager and to help dissipate the fog of uncertainty that surrounds his future. We see a promising future for them and pass along this message in a consistent and authentic way, in the hope that our belief will allow them to use their 'dream muscle' and to march toward that better future.

In one of our educational communities in the periphery of Israel, following a session on 'anchors in the future,' the women of the staff organized a tour of a local vocational college for the school's junior class. The Village Way facilitator who joined the tour explained:

"The majority of these students do not finish high school. The tour happened just before spring break, and it was the first attempt of its kind to connect them to higher education. We waited with anticipation for this meeting. We knew that if it was successful, it might encourage the students to see academic studies as relevant to them. On the other hand, if this meeting was a failure, it would have the opposite effect.

At first it seemed like a total failure! The first college student we met spoke condescendingly, using pretentious language that went way over their heads. The juniors' body language testified to the fact that they were not emotionally present at that meeting; they were totally focused on their cellphones or on each other. The homeroom teacher and I looked at one another with frustration and felt that our biggest fear had come true. Fortunately, the meeting with the next student was completely different. A young woman responsible for all the certification studies at the college entered the room. She told the young people about the successes of the college, about the different professions they could acquire, and about the famous alumni that had come from that area and had achieved success. "All that you have to do in order for this to happen to you," she said, "is just to finish high school." Slowly the juniors began to wake up, listen and ask questions. She answered them directly, making the message and the academic experience more accessible to them. She showed them that it would be possible for them to obtain a profession that would let them make an honest living. Suddenly, it seemed possible. They understood that this was something

that they were capable of, that they too could go to college and succeed.
You could see they were going back to the image of their future
that the homeroom teacher built with them, toward meaningful
'anchors in the future.' It also had a positive impact on learning
in the classroom and led most of the students to finish high school."

Just as the possibility of higher education in the future became achievable in the eyes of these students, we must help the young people in our lives dream, imagine and tangibly sense their hopes for the future. Our challenge as educators is to allow them to touch the future, to get to know the possibilities, to deepen their familiarity with it and to feel capable of succeeding. The life stories of someone they know or can relate to help them create 'anchors in the future.' We have an opportunity to help the student build a meaningful and positive plan for the future, and in doing so, influence the 'timeline' of their lives.

We need to develop the ability to see from a bird's eye view, to show youth what we see for them in their future. We are all afraid of the unknown, but as veterans of adolescence who are living our own lives, it is important that we serve as an island of stability. Fear of the unknown sometimes turns into the desire to live in the moment and can lead to dysfunctional behaviors. If we can lift the fog of an unknown future, we can make it easier on them and us.

Often, the adults in the educational community serve as a source of inspiration for the future, as examples of people who have come a long way in the world and who are experienced in handling crossroads, choices, failures and successes. Adva, a graduate of a Village Way educational community, told me how her educators' past experience affected her perception of her own future:

I remember that when I was a senior, there was an "employment week"
held at school, in which we thought we would talk about possible
professions for the future. To us, it sounded both boring and far off. I

will never forget the surprise when I came into the school hallway at the beginning of the week and saw that it was decorated with life stories, and not just any stories, our educators' life stories. Every educator outlined the path he or she took from high school until they found their calling. There were pictures of the different periods of their lives, crossroads of deliberation, drawings of obstacles along the way—in short, their life path. It was intriguing, funny and interesting. In retrospect, I realize how significant it was. We, the students, were asked to explore the different life stories and pick the one that we were most interested in learning more about. I chose to explore the path of my physical education teacher who I really liked. What most impressed me was that she told us it took her a long time to understand what she wanted, and she addressed the various stages she went through in the process of arriving where she was. I also remember she told us how she met her husband and what else she hoped to achieve. If I am not mistaken, she wanted to develop a method combining sports with academic studies. When I completed my military service and was deliberating what to study, this experience stuck with me. I feel that I understood from her that we are constantly evolving, and that at every stage we can decide again what and how to be.

Drawing a Picture of the Future—Positive or Realistic?

Educators face a real difficulty—presenting a picture of an optimistic future while a teen's current actions may seem to lead to a negative one. In the face of this difficulty, we require extensive humility and patience. We must remember the stories of those who succeeded despite great challenges, or of graduates whose journeys to success passed through such stages, and then—expose the kids to these stories. As said, the future affects the present.

It is crucial that we refresh the conversation, that we surprise teens with a positive attitude that is not guided by their momentary choice of something negative, but instead creates an energizing change in direction. It is equally important that we pay attention to youth who, despite their best efforts, do not appear to experience enough success. Am I deceiving a teenager when I encourage him to strive for success, but I feel he cannot really reach it?

Teenagers need to be encouraged to strive, to dream and to paint a picture of an optimistic future. This requires us to return to the place of "I don't know everything," and ask ourselves: Is what I currently think to be impossible for this young person actually impossible? Sometimes we think that in order to be realistic, we should curtail our optimism. For every one of our educational actions, there are costs and consequences. We will never know the best future for a young person, if indeed one exists. There will always be those students whom it is easy to assist in imagining a future, and those about whom we will remain unsure. When we are unsure, we must choose between the sin of discouragement, which creates a supposedly realistic picture of the future while lowering expectations, and the sin of delusion, which creates an optimistic picture of the future but risks causing disappointment for the individual. Given these choices, I wholeheartedly choose the sin of delusion. Discouraging a youngster may cause her to aim lower than she can reach, due to my own possibly mistaken assessment.

In a lecture that psychologist Victor Frankl gave to students in Toronto in 1972[14], he explained why we should believe in a person's abilities far beyond what we can see. He showed how important this is for fulfilling the hidden potential that lies in every person. Frankl said that during his pilot training, the flight instructor explained how to make navigational adjustments due to crosswinds. If a pilot wants to reach an airport at a specific point in the east while there is a north wind blowing, he must navigate as if he is flying to a destination located north of the airport in order to offset the effect of the wind on the plane. To reach a destination, the pilot must direct the plane to a much further destination. How does this relate to humans and a life of meaning? Frankl used the

14   Viktor E. Frankl "Youth in Search of Meaning Speech" (St. Michael's College, University of Toronto, Ontario, Canada, 1972).

words of the philosopher Goethe: "Treat a man as he is, and you make him worse than he is. Treat a man as he ought to be and you help him become who he is capable of being."

We are at a staff meeting for educators doing student assessments for 11th-grade students. We get to Joseph. The history teacher sighs: "He doesn't have an ounce of responsibility, that guy." The other teachers nod. "When he finally comes to class, it's without his notebook or books, almost always late," another teacher says. His housemother adds that in his home he does not complete his chores. His homeroom teacher says that for the past week, he has not even showed up for school. The director of the youth village moves uncomfortably in his chair and asks: "Does anyone have anything else to add about Joseph?" And then his informal educator, who helps the students during downtime, says: "Usually I agree with what has been said about Joseph, but last week I got to know a whole different kid. As you know, his friend Moshe has been having a hard time at home—his family was declaring bankruptcy, and they were in a terrible place. During the past week, while Moshe helped his parents with bureaucracy, it was his friend Joseph who stepped in to take care of the younger siblings and run the household, making sure there was food in the fridge and that the kids were okay. Moshe said he doesn't know how his family would have gotten through that time without Joseph."

The history teacher knows Joseph from class, a place where she is expected to pass on knowledge and study habits, and she sees his lack of personal responsibility. She sees Joseph exactly as he presents himself to her. Goethe, however, suggests treating Joseph as he is capable of being, according to his potential, despite the inherent difficulty. The director of the youth village sought to zoom out and see the wider frame. He understood that not all staff members see the same side of Joseph. No person is one-dimensional. Sometimes students choose not to let us get to know every side of them, either due to a lack of trust or past experiences of disappointment. Considering what the informal educator shared, the history teacher's words begin to lose importance. Joseph is a very responsible person, although he still behaves irresponsibly towards his studies. Now the whole team will be able to treat him as a young man who can be trusted and who can take responsibility. When he is treated this way by the supportive adults in the village, he will probably be able to better fulfill his potential.

We all want to be supportive adults serving a significant role in the life of a child, although our busy daily routine may make that difficult. Offering ongoing support to students begins from the top and is the responsibility of each adult. A principal who treats staff as they deserve to be treated will also help them to see the teenagers as they might one day be, not as they are at one moment in time. It is my hope and wish that we succeed in including a mechanism in our system for sharing the good things, which will help us nurture students to reach their goals.

No Dreams in a Vacuum

When young people lack a positive picture of the future, an image emerges from a desperate reality; one in which a teenager is influenced by older neighborhood friends or family members who sit at home without doing anything or take advantage of others for their own personal gain. This is a tangible picture of the future that causes the teenager to say to himself: *I am probably going to be like them.* It is extremely difficult to create optimistic dreams in a vacuum. As educators, we are often faced with a powerful picture of the future demonstrated in a young person's difficult reality, and yet we keep believing that a teacher or parent who promises a better future can help. However, just making such promises will not work.

It is imperative that we introduce adolescents to adults who came from the same environment as they did and have succeeded, thus allowing the student to question their beliefs about their own futures. "Here is something I can see and believe, hold on to and feel, the neighbor or the student from the year above me, who I remember as drinking and smoking almost as much as I do, is different now! He succeeded, studied at a preparatory gap-year program, served in a meaningful position in the Israeli army, and is now studying at college. Hey, it is possible that I could do it too."

A supportive adult can, just by being him or herself, help students to strengthen their 'anchors in the past and future.' Personal stories can influence students' openness to rethinking their past and future. The personal stories of graduates can be even more effective in this regard. By using the stories of educators and graduates, one can depict the future, not as a finish line, but as a learning process with multiple steps along the way.

Can You Dream for Someone Else?

As an educator myself, I have put this advice into practice, but it hasn't always led to the desired outcome. I have exposed students to many different possible pictures of the future. I have asked them constantly: "What do you want to be when you grow up? What do want to do when you graduate?" I have told them: "You are going to be leaders, so let's work on your leadership skills." I have done everything recommended, and sometimes, they just did not respond to it. They did nothing that would advance them. They did not take any of the active steps that would allow them to be accepted to positive post-high school programs. They simply went wherever the wind took them. But even in such cases, all hope is not lost.

Sarit lived in an Israeli 'development town' in the country's geographic and socioeconomic periphery. In the building where she lived, there was an apartment of college students who were studying to be teachers. She saw them as particularly important figures and shared with me how influential they had been on the people in her apartment building. We offered 11th grade students guidance workshops in which the students were asked what they wanted to do after they graduated. Some answers were very general, and there were also some specific answers about what role they wanted to be when they were older. Sarit said that she wanted to study. I told her, "Great, but there are a lot of options of where and what to study. Maybe you want to study education?" And she said: "What? Me? A teacher?!" When I had almost given up, she suddenly said: "Why do you think they would accept me to a teaching certificate program?" I understood then that this was something Sarit did not even think was an option for her.

Over time, we continued to consider the idea while talking about other options as well. Just before the winter holidays during her senior year, we brought in school graduates to talk to the students, among them a teacher. Three teenagers were interested in the topic, but Sarit stayed out of the conversation. The others signed up for entrance examinations to the teacher certification program, but Sarit did not. I told her that she should sign up and try out, and that when she got accepted, she could then decide. Sarit did not cooperate, so I started pushing even more. I called her into my office and together we made a phone call to register her for the entrance exams. The evening before the exam we did some simulation exercises to prepare for the test. Sarit came but did not cooperate.

The thought that a young woman in her senior year of high school was still unwilling to do anything for her future was disappointing to me. Unfortunately, Sarit was not alone. Many like her were not able to get it together because of low self-esteem and a lack of confidence. More than once, I thought, maybe it is time to say: "You made your bed; now lie in it." But I decided not to give up on Sarit. Every day, at different opportunities, I would say to her: "You are going to be a teacher." Even when Sarit would say: "You'll see, I won't even get in." I would respond, "Yes, you will. And if not, it will be because they failed to truly get to know you and not because you don't deserve it. And in that case, we will appeal the process and help them to get

to know you better." Ultimately, Sarit got into the teacher training
program, and two years later, she came to the school to talk to seniors
about her profession and about the process it took to get her there.

We are obligated to do a great deal to help teenagers dream, aspire and develop 'images of the future.' That includes the possibility of dreaming for them—sometimes even against their stated will—aiming for the place where they deserve to be. It can seem a drastic step to plan another person's future. According to what criteria do we direct a person to an outcome that he did not choose—our values, wishes, even our whims? How is that any different than parents and teachers who are trying to vicariously fulfill their personal dreams through their children or students, and in doing so harm the youngster's capability for self-realization? To me, there is a difference. The main task for those who lack ambition is to develop and strengthen the 'muscle' of ambition. It is important to help this process occur at the beginning of the educational process and then return to it and invest in it over time. When we reach crunch time, we do not have the luxury to play by all the rules. There is a principle in Jewish law that makes it permissible to act contrary to the stated laws of the Torah in a moment of existential crisis for the Jewish people. For our purposes as educators, this means there are situations in which we need to temporarily break the rules because the intended purpose of those rules is best met by doing so. It is not ideal to dream for a student, but in certain situations, it is right to do so. On rare occasions, it is even appropriate to make a decision for him or her.

It is likely that for every young person like Sarit who benefited from the fact that we decided for them, there will be some for whom it was not right. At Yemin Orde, we encourage our students to attend gap-year and community service programs. While we believe this is the right step for most of them, there will still be those for whom such programs are not suitable. We need to try to help those students choose an alternative that suits them, but in no way should the majority be denied the possibility of meaningful encouragement due to the minority.

Just as 'anchors in the past' affect the present and future, so 'anchors in the future' affect the present and change the past. In many cases, there is a self-perception rooted in the past in which the teenager feels he is not worthy of succeeding. By offering trust and introducing him to success stories and the expectations of the educational community, we may help change this, and with it, his whole concept of time. He may even begin to dream and work to fulfill those dreams.

With You All the Way

'With You All the Way:' *A Response to the Fear of Being Alone*

"With You All the Way" is a motto of Village Way educational communities. The essential emotional message is: "We are with you; you have unconditional, supportive social and communal relationships. We are here with you and believe in you—now as a student and in the future as our graduate. We offer you support as part of your social and economic safety net, and we are part of your network for leveraging opportunities. We are a key component in your toolbox."

Fear of the unknown is connected to the primordial fear of being alone, and it causes significant anxiety among teenagers. Often, in the final years of school, the students who previously went through a meaningful educational process are the ones who begin to fall apart. The fear of tomorrow and the concern that their educational community might not be there for them intensifies, leading them to disengage. They have had their fill of goodbyes and abandonment in their young lives. We, the educators, may also have feelings of fear for their future. A graduate's encounter with a difficult commanding officer in the military or an overly tough boss at a new job has the potential to send a years-long educational process down the drain unless the young person has an additional support system to help process the experience and learn how to cope. It often seems that the educational process is like the battle for a rebound ball in a basketball game. Someone needs to catch the wayward student and return her to the right side of the game for another chance, before she leaves the court or goes over to the other team.

Our promise of a meaningful relationship is reflected in our commitment to remain by our students' side in the future. The knowledge that we will always be with them, should they need it, reduces anxiety and gives them confidence to face challenges. Educational communities cannot continue to support every graduate at the end of their studies, and the truth is that not all graduates require this kind of guidance, yet, it is both appropriate and realistic to ask educators to be available to provide help, wherever possible, to those graduates who do need it. Supporting alumni can be added to the educational community's long to-do list and should be prioritized among all the required tasks.

The Long Goodbye: *Dealing with Transitions*

What happens to students just before the end of senior year? Just when they should be enjoying the fruits of this shared journey, we see some students not really functioning and beginning to evade responsibility. Thoughts about saying goodbye and finishing school are all mixed up with concerns for the next step and the fear of taking it. In a conversation in the teachers' lounge, a colleague shared with me that there was an "end-of-year feeling" in his class; that they were relaxed, taking it easy, and they could no longer focus on their studies. I told him I was familiar with this feeling, but that in my opinion, they were not relaxed but actually more stressed out. The stress of an unknown future had overtaken any sense of self-discipline and commitment to their studies.

When spring comes, the twelfth-grade educators get antsy. The sense that we need to hold the students on a short leash so they do not get lost may overpower everything else. Educators are also tired; saying goodbye to another class is not always easy. We need to be prepared for the effects of transitional periods, and not be surprised by them every time they arise.

The students with whom we had the most meaningful relationships and who went through the most promising processes are usually the ones who have trouble finishing school properly. They test us to see whether we are going to give up on them at the last minute, or stand by their side when they need it, as we promised.

Karen, a senior, got a small part in the end-of-year play. She was incredibly happy, and I overheard her on the phone asking her older sister to tell her Mom to attend the show. As the evening grew closer, the pressure and excitement grew. We tried to keep a proper balance between study sessions for finals and rehearsals for the show. The night before the big show, there was a dress rehearsal. Everyone was in place and ready on time; only Karen was missing. The director of the show asked everyone to go look for her. Karen arrived 20 minutes late and immediately got yelled at for her lateness. The faculty member directing the show threatened: "One more problem with you tonight and you won't go onstage. Your part is short; we can find a replacement." Karen was hurt but would not let it show. She almost responded rudely but chose not to. But when the time came for her to get on stage for the rehearsal, she did not go on. The director said into the microphone: "Karen, you are ruining this for everyone, again. You are not performing tonight. We will find a replacement."

I approached the director of the show and tried to remind him that the kids were stressed and that while it was important the performance be a success, the real reason for our being there was not to produce wonderful shows. I said I understood where he was coming from and the frustration, he must have felt that the kids were not behaving seriously and respectfully. But I reminded him, The Village Way concept of not giving up on a young person applied in this case as well. I explained that I would speak with Karen and make it clear to her that her behavior was unacceptable, but that she would be allowed to perform.

The director got angry and felt his authority was being compromised. After some discussion, he eventually was convinced that my plan was the right thing to do. After all, on previous occasions, he had been the one to persuade us to allow kids with behavior problems to get on stage, so as not to prevent them from having experiences of success. We both had the same goals for the students. The real challenge now was to convince Karen to get on stage. She was hurt and said she would not participate if they didn't want her. With the help of her friends and informal educator, she did end up performing.

What happens to us, both adults and teenagers, just before transitions? Like Karen in the story, we sometimes run away and refuse to deal with them. Our teens need us to be in a nurturing place that prevents them from escaping. We must learn to cope, to say goodbye respectfully—neither slamming the door nor closing the gate on the other before the end. In these situations, it helps to send the message through word and actions that the students are not alone, that we will continue to keep in touch, even if at a different level.

Yearbook Photo

Over the course of a month, Avi, the senior homeroom teacher, took it upon himself to take charge of the yearbook photos. Two days of photography shoots at school were scheduled. Those who could not make it had to go to the photographer's studio. Everyone posed for their photos in white shirts, as is customary for celebratory occasions in Israel—everyone except for Yael and Amnon. Yael did not get her picture taken at all, and Amnon deliberately showed up for the photo session in a black shirt. On the last day, Avi announced that these two students would not appear in the yearbook photos. He reasoned that they were old enough, and he should not have to chase after them to take an appropriate picture. Avi certainly had approached them many times to remind them, but I felt it was wrong to give up on them. While not everyone places a lot of importance on the yearbook, not appearing in it could leave a lasting negative sense about one's school years. I called Levi, a talented friend of Yael and Amnon, and asked him for help. He came right away. I asked him to find a picture of Yael from the database of pictures taken over the year, to use Photoshop to digitally place a white shirt onto her image and to adjust it to the proper size. He did so willingly and sent the picture to the photographer. As for Amnon, the photographer saw Yael's photo, and took it upon himself to change Amnon's black shirt to a white one using Photoshop.

Investing in Graduates Bears Fruit

Dr. Chaim Peri used to say: "Every shekel that we invest in a graduate is worth 10 shekels invested in a student." One example of many is Worko's story.

Worko, a tenth-grade student, had a rebellious nature, and at every opportunity would announce that he would not be enlisting in the military, which is mandatory in Israel after high school. The head of social services at the Village decided to take him to the ceremony marking one of the Village graduate's completion of an officer course. On the way, Worko told her: "When I finish officer training, you will also come to my graduation." The price of travel to the officer's army base was worth 10 times more as it greatly impacted Worko's image of his future.

Connection with alumni not only benefits the alumni, but also creates an important, consistent message for current students. For them, the graduates are role models, and meeting with them allows students to develop an 'image of the future,' preparing them for future options and planting the seeds of the idea that they can do it too. In addition, the graduates are living proof that the Village community will remain present for the current students all the way.

Haviv had been among the most challenging kids in school, and we were all concerned about how he would handle college life. The only child of a single mother, he had no siblings or father to share stories with him or to prepare him for higher education. Although his college graduation ceremony took place far from the Village, there was no way we could pass up the opportunity to be by his side for the event. We called his mother to offer her a ride, and she happily accepted, explaining that she had debated whether to attend because her medical condition meant public transportation was out of the question. We travelled together, three teachers with Haviv's mother and some student representatives. The ceremony was very impressive, and we were excited to see Haviv, our graduate and now, a college graduate as well. For some of the students, this was their first time attending any kind of college graduation. They were excited to see their friend achieving such an important milestone.

Seeing Haviv after the ceremony produced overwhelming joy. He had no idea that we were coming and had prepared himself for the possibility that no one would come to support him, even going so far as to plan to join one of the other families. When he saw his mother and us, he was so excited that he hugged everyone and shook his head in disbelief. For a long time, he looked at everyone with a smile plastered on his face. The meaning of "with you all the way" spread through all of us in full force. Haviv felt that we were with him and would continue to be with him. Although he had already graduated high school and even completed college, he was still part of the community. The students who had joined us saw what the future might hold for them and were reassured of our continued support for them in the life events to come. We felt gratified watching Haviv the college grad hugging his mother.

Graduate support is an integral part of 'anchors in the future' for the entire educational community. Temporal anchors—past and future—are established by consistently building confidence while referencing the personal or communal past along with a message regarding the future: *We believe that you will succeed and are with you all the way.* Anchors in the past and future stem from meaningful relationships with supportive adults and from a deep, mutual feeling of belonging. The educational community itself becomes a significant 'anchor' in the lives of those who are educated within it, supporting them through their various stages of growth.

What About a Graduate who is a Negative Role Model?

> *Danny was a young graduate of Yemin Orde who had a positive experience in his mandatory military service and then returned to his neighborhood. His return brought with it a reversion to old habits: using drugs, drinking alcohol, and not doing much else. Danny was involved in a violent brawl that, by some miracle, only ended in bruises. He was then suspected of attempting to stab someone and was detained for two days, after which he was put under house arrest for the duration of the legal proceedings. When Danny's house was found unsuitable for house arrest, the educational staff at Yemin Orde began debating whether to allow Danny to stay in the Youth Village Graduates' Home during his house arrest.*

The discussion was complicated. The educators brought up the question of whether it was wise to expose students to Danny as a potential model for their future. Many also had safety concerns. On the other hand, the graduate coordinator reminded us of the idea of "with you all the way," and its importance especially in moments of crisis, not only for those graduates in whom we can easily take pride. One of the social workers reminded us that some students are 'late bloomers,' adolescents who take more time to adapt, thrive, and achieve independence. Yet another educator added that the law enforcement authorities were allowing house arrest, and our campus would be acceptable in that context, with the only remaining option being jail.

Over the course of the discussion, we dealt with the question of how this might influence current students. What would they gain from this story? Would they be influenced by Danny's drinking, violence and hurting others or would they internalize the staff's code of conduct and understand that we really stand by the principle of "with you all the way"—even if you stray? In the end, Danny came to the Village for alternative detention and was eventually rehabilitated. In this case, it worked out. But we have had other instances in which alternative detention at our village has prompted struggles, and therefore each case must be judged on its own. Many of our students and graduates are not open to learning or complex self-development during their adolescence. They must first get through adolescence safely, and only then, can they bloom in the next stage. Our presence in their lives after high school years allows them to grow in the right direction and to flourish at a later stage. Sometimes our presence in their lives allows us to witness this and draw enormous strength from it.

The relationship between students and educators within an educational community is not timebound. A student who is a real member of a community remains a member even after graduation. There is a connection rooted in deep belonging among graduates of our educational communities. Offering support through crises, celebrations, and transitions, and developing programs for empowering graduates are integral tasks of an educational community.

During adolescence, it is crucial to work with the 'timeline,' and to channel the powerful force inherent in one's perception of the past and the future. A supportive educator and a meaningful educational community guide the students in channeling the power of the 'timeline,' with significant 'anchors' in the personal, communal, and cultural past and future.

Graduates Day

Yemin Orde Youth Village developed the tradition of an event called Graduates Day, now also held at many Village Way educational communities. Graduates studying in institutions of higher education across Israel come to the Village and meet with students in small groups, sharing their past experiences, including the challenges they face and the reasons for choosing their path. Everyone eats dinner together and there is a scholarship-granting ceremony in the evening.

This day has three objectives:

- Recognizing the graduates for persistence and accomplishment in reaching higher education
- Helping our current students develop a variety of attainable 'images of the future'
- Encouraging the staff to draw strength from the fruits of their labor: The educational staff members deal with difficulties on a regular basis, and this brief respite allows them to see graduates who did not always make it easy and have now turned into success stories. Behind every one of these graduates stands a staff member who refused to break down or give up.

Graduates Day is a rest stop that lets us recharge in the spirit of Psalm 110:7: "He drinks from the stream on his way; therefore he holds his head high"[15] The importance of resting along the way is well-known, but do we remember to create points of rest and to take the time to stop at them and refuel?

The Past, the Future, and Cultural Heritage

The 'past-future timeline' exists in cultural, communal and societal contexts, and each student's perception of his 'timeline' influences his identity. Personal and collective memories are essential for constructing identity; they influence a person substantially—his values, worldview

---

15   *The Holy Scriptures: The New JPS Translation according to the Traditional Hebrew Text* Philadelphia PA, 1985, in Sefaria.com

and self-perception. A key part of the curriculum in history and other social studies topics relates to the communal narrative and 'anchors in the past and future.' However, attention is not always paid to the student's cultural heritage, and sometimes, an essential conflict arises between this personal culture and the mainstream culture. In negotiating the 'timeline' and 'anchors in the past and future,' students may have to reconcile various circles of identity. The educational community, with its multiplicity of cultures, religions and denominations, should consciously and respectfully relate to the cultural heritage of its students. Dealing with one's cultural heritage is a meaningful practice for students. Doing so will prepare them for a future in which various value systems may clash, so that they will be able to sort through them and create a path that is exactly right for them.

What's Your Ethnic Group?

As mentioned, our perception of reality lies in experiences that we have translated into thoughts regarding our environment and ourselves—our worldview. This is as true for students as it is for educators. As educators, our attitude towards our students' background has a decisive impact on the way in which the student perceives his future. Indeed, as educators it is difficult to talk about the effect of students' personal-cultural pasts, and how those shape the present and the future, without taking an honest look at our own personal-cultural pasts. The way in which we remember our past, and our role in it, has led us to a certain worldview and educational approach. For example, the way in which I understand the issue of personal-cultural past in education is deeply rooted in my experiences as a child, as a teenager, and as a young man.

> *I grew up in the town of Bat Yam, near Tel Aviv. My older brother was born in a ma'abara, an immigrant transit camp, and I was born a short time after my parents moved to a nearby housing project. My extended family stayed in the ma'abara, so I spent much of my childhood there. The culture of my childhood included a whole*

spectrum of experiences, smells, tastes, melodies, prayers and customs. In the years when I was growing up, there was an extensive national debate surrounding ethnicity, particularly as it pertained to Mizrachi Jews, who hail from the Middle East and North Africa (as opposed to Ashkenazi Jews, who descend from European Jews). The national discourse at the time ranged from allegations of discrimination and deprivation made by prominent Mizrachim, to sketch comedy skits and jokes. My parents built a happy and peaceful life incorporating our family and ethnic Mizrachi traditions. They chose not to allow conversations about deprivation and discrimination into our house. The narrative they supported was completely different. They expressed pride in our heritage and felt a responsibility to maintain an ancient tradition alongside faith in our family's power to innovate from within it. The warm and trusting environment of our home, the belief in our abilities, and the strong feeling of belonging became anchors in my life and in the lives of my brothers and sisters, and they accompany us as touchpoints of strength, and confidence.

At school and in youth movement events I attended, there were kids from diverse homes, but the culture I encountered in those places was a unitary one. In the public sphere, there was little reflection of the traditions of our homes, except for a few ethnic dishes that everyone loved. The message that was conveyed, even if unintentionally, was that cultural diversity was not legitimate, that celebrating one's own heritage made one "not Israeli enough." Thus, despite the sense of warmth and safety I received at home, there were things of which I was ashamed. I recall that I developed strong reservations regarding Arabic music and about being loud or expressive, which I associated with Mizrachi celebrations and family traditions. I do not know fully where that reticence came from, and I think it would be superficial to attribute it just to the lack of representation of diverse cultures in the various educational systems in which I was educated. It could be that it was also part of a natural process of rejection of the world of adults,

a typical element in finding one's own way. Of course, doing things
differently than one's parents is fine. There is room for a teenager to
reject parts of his cultural heritage, but only when this is carried out
from a place of real choice and not out of shame.

Today, I want to believe that if a teenager were to decide to reject a certain
component of his family worldview or heritage, I would not just accept it
as the natural way of the world, but would be attentive to it. It is integral
that there be more educators and supportive adults in schools and youth
movements who give voice to the unique beauty of every heritage and
create a public space to express different cultures.

In addition to addressing the personal past, it is important to connect
to the cultural past, in which there are also strong 'anchors' that can have
an impact on a young person's life. An educational system that does not
allow for the expression of the diverse cultural heritages of its students and
treats the students as one-dimensional may create cognitive dissonance.

It is the role of the skilled educator to find the strengths from within
a cultural heritage. Just as we should know the names and basic background
information of every one of our students, so too, should we understand
the cultural sources that impact his identity. Developing familiarity with
different cultures is essential to our professional development, and our
ability to provide an accurate response to our students.

We are presented with opportunities for learning all the time. A
sensitive, interested and curious educator can do this through direct
encounters with the students, as well as through formal class opportunities.
This can be achieved with a culturally relevant picture hanging in the
classroom, an exhibit of ethnic objects, or quotes from different cultures
and languages decorating the school hallways. This learning can take place
during teacher training days, through sessions that enrich knowledge of
different cultural heritages, as well as in the classroom. In places like Israel
and the US, the immense diversity can make it difficult to familiarize
ourselves with all the different cultures and there may always be a gap in

our knowledge. However, our willingness to learn is important and enables connection to begin. The more interest we show, the more we can narrow the gaps and increase the possibility of equal treatment for each child.

The Swan Effect

Dr. Wovit Worko and other graduates of Yemin Orde talk about their experience as students who came to study in a youth village that valued their cultural heritage as a formative experience. The same sense of belonging for which Ethiopian Israelis marched thousands of miles to reach *Eretz Israel* (the Land of Israel) was reinforced in the educational community. This is how she tells it:

> *"The framework of the Village made it possible to absorb every immigrant who came. The educators knew the culture from which each boy and girl came and encouraged us to recognize and be proud of the culture. The educators knew about our traditional holiday, the Sigd festival; they celebrated with us. We felt that there was room for our tradition, from prayers to activities and foods. We were taught that our culture and language were an asset. Anyone who wanted to, could speak Amharic and even study toward a matriculation grade in Amharic."*[16]

Another graduate shared:

> *"I came to the educational community as an Ethiopian immigrant after every other place I had been had given me the feeling that I was a burden on society. In the opening conversation, I heard the village director saying, 'The Ethiopian Jews are the sons of kings.' And then I heard the concepts I had heard many times from my parents about preserving Jewish identity and practical Zionism. Later in the*

remarks, I heard the director say: 'How good it is that Israeli society has been able to witness its brothers' return!'"

The swan in the story of Hans Christian Anderson's *The Ugly Duckling* recognizes he is a swan only after those surrounding him see his beauty and admire him. Only then, does he look back at his reflection from the lake and see himself as a swan. Children who feel that there is something ugly in them, or what they represent, have difficulty seeing themselves as they really are. We, as educators, need to see what is beautiful in them and their heritage—which is an essential part of them—and show them that we admire it. We must make them find the good in themselves.

Cultural Mediation and Communal Values

As mentioned, I have sometimes screened *The Lion King* for my high school students. The movie is about a lion cub becoming the king of the animals. For students, it serves as a trigger for discussion about leadership, running away from responsibility, fears, strengths and weaknesses. With one of my classes, I chose to show this movie, assuming a cartoon would make the lesson a bit lighter, more interesting and refreshing, but I was not prepared for my students' response—they expressed complete opposition in every possible way to watching the movie. When I asked them about it, I realized that they were offended. The choice to show a cartoon was interpreted in their minds as completely disrespectful. Most of the young people felt that bringing in a children's movie was showing disregard for their actual age. My explanation regarding the more adult messages conveyed by the movie was not accepted.

For my students, the cartoon film was added to a long list of experiences in which they felt they were not being treated as adults. A teenager may be convinced that he can drink and smoke or come home late at night since he is already mature, and it is important for him to maintain that self-image. Taking this into consideration, I take special care dealing with youth who have immigrated to Israel and do not have a full grasp of Hebrew yet. I make a special effort not to talk down to them just because I am speaking in simple language. The wish to be seen as competent was apparent to me as one young immigrant student left my class in anger, saying: "I don't know Hebrew, but I am not stupid!" As educators we need to develop the ability to convey complex messages in a simple way without giving up on the nuances, to find a way to talk and to teach at an appropriately high level using simple terminology.

I had used the cartoon film in youth groups and with high school seniors many times, and I had never come across kids who were offended. Such a response is dependent on the hearts and minds of the students. In general, if they feel more confident and appreciated, they will likely become open to a new experience they may initially perceive as childish.

In the framework of our educator training sessions, I met Benny, an educator and Bible teacher at a religious high school. The purpose of the meeting was to prepare lesson plans that would strengthen the students' feeling of belonging. During the meeting, the school's Bible coordinator, who also happens to be the coordinator of the lesson plans, arrived and asked if Benny would fill in as a substitute teacher in the Hebrew class for immigrants. Benny asked if he was supposed to teach a certain topic and the coordinator gave him illustrated worksheets on the weekly Torah portion. Seeing the worksheets, we looked at one another and smiled—they were worksheets for young children, the same ones our kids bring home from kindergarten or first grade.

Benny smiled and said to the coordinator: "Are you serious? These are worksheets for little kids. They are 17-year-olds!" "True," said the coordinator, "but this is exactly suited to their level of knowledge of both Hebrew and Bible." Benny and I felt uncomfortable and wondered whether the students would accept these worksheets with easy curiosity or see them as an insult. I told Benny my experience with the movie *The Lion King,* and we understood that we would have to introduce the worksheets differently. On the one hand, they really did match their learning level; but on the other hand, they did not match their age and maturity level.

We decided to approach the topic by talking to the students about the importance of quality time with their younger siblings. We encouraged them to find time to study with their siblings, with the understanding that their parents who don't speak Hebrew cannot help their children with homework. After the conversation, we suggested they take the worksheets and work on them together with their younger siblings before Shabbat. But first, we would go over the worksheets together and answer any questions to make sure that they would be properly prepared to help their siblings. From an embarrassing situation that would have been interpreted as insulting, we turned it around to a win-win. We taught material that was adjusted to their language level, and at the same time, were able to inspire meaningful learning. Some of them came back and talked with great satisfaction about working with their siblings.

When Cultural Codes Clash

Language and cultural codes have a major impact on basic communication. Understanding anchors in the past alongside cultural codes assists the students in perceiving the difference between conduct familiar to them and that which is accepted in the society into which they are integrating. They can then decide for themselves what is important for them. Hopefully, this negotiation will become an 'anchor in their past,' which will help them in various ways.

Over the years, we have become familiar with the customs and cultural codes of the students. For example, students who immigrated to Israel from the Caucasus region refused to take their turn to clean the communal toilets and always tried to avoid it or trade their turn with others. When their informal educator finally said she would do it since no one else would, they were confused because her decision went against the code of respect for authority figures they had learned at home. A lot of time and patience was required for us to find common ground on the issue.

Another example involves hand gestures. A gesture in which the forefinger and thumb make a circle and the three remaining fingers remain straight means "OK" in some cultures, while in others it suggests a zero or a negative. Thus, was born the entertaining skit by the famous comedic duo Yossi and Shmuel about a father that comes to a parent-teacher meeting and the teacher signs with her hands that she thinks the girl is a great student. The father, on the other hand, understands from the hand gesture that his daughter is seen as a loser and gets angry at the teacher. The sketch is funny but suggests a painful reality.

Similarly, many educators and Israeli army officers have had conversations with students and soldiers of Ethiopian descent who would not look them in the eye. Often this behavior raised suspicions that the student was not telling the truth or did not respect the person standing in front of him, when in fact, the downward gaze was a sign of respect. From the Ethiopian perspective, such a young person is showing respect for authority by not looking the individual in the eye—while the educator or officer may believe he is being treated with distrust or contempt.

So, what do we do? We start with the important understanding that the way each one of us interprets things is neither correct nor incorrect. Not everything we see and hear is what others are trying to communicate. I may feel hurt, but it does not mean that someone was trying to hurt me. If certain speech seems to indicate rudeness, there is a high probability that the student is being rude, but it could also be that he did not intend it that way. This is especially true for conversations between adults and teenagers with different cultural codes because added to the intercultural encounter is also the perennial generational gap.

The next step requires we get to know our students, their world, and their cultural and moral codes. Obviously, we cannot learn everything, but it is important to remember that there are other components to communication. As educators, we should ask if there was something that we did not necessarily understand. We then facilitate this process for adolescents who are dealing with new cultural environments.

As an educator, I share with young people that others will not always properly understand their behavior. I pass on the responsibility to them, to examine their habits, and to understand that if they speak or gesture in a certain way, a person unfamiliar with their habits may respond in a way that does not match their intention. This requires them to consider how to be better understood. When cultural codes collide, the responsibility for understanding and cooperation is on both sides, but the initial responsibility is usually on the adult or the person for whom the dominant culture is more familiar.

> When I was a homeroom teacher for a 12th grade class, I would play a game with the students where we would stand in a circle and pass a ball to one another, but only after making eye contact. In the framework of the game, it was acceptable to look straight into someone's eyes. I wasn't trying to change my students' cultural codes of respect but to practice the game of life in Israel, where a direct gaze is crucial. I sought to help them broaden the possibilities for styles of communication from which they could choose. I share that not everyone sees averting one's eyes as an expression of respect, and that there are those for whom such a reaction may even trigger anger.

When Values Clash

Sometimes it seems that different groups hold entirely different values, but after broadening our knowledge, it becomes clear that many values are actually shared, but have different external expressions. Take, for example, the story of eye contact with the army officer. In both cultural styles, there is a shared value of respect for authority. In one culture, this is expressed by avoiding the authority figure's gaze, and in another, by listening accompanied with eye contact. In this situation, the conflict appears complex, but once we understand that the value is shared, it is relatively easy to solve.

However, when it comes to social norms that are in stark opposition to those accepted in Israeli society, it becomes more challenging. How do we handle the role of women in conservative societies, marriages under the age of 18, violence under the guise of family honor, and other conflicts? If there are no serious consequences, we can allow the ethical dispute to exist. But when values or norms of a certain culture go against the law, we need to be in line with the law. The Israeli legislature has set down laws that allow for the protection of values that enable us to live together. Therefore, when the law is violated, we must take an unequivocal position. It is important to share with our students a significant complex principle: *I understand but I do not agree.* I can understand a person that acts a certain way because that is how he was raised and how it was acceptable in his environment, but I am not obligated to agree with him. In fact, in cases that are against the law, I am obliged to disagree with him, even as I am not exempt from understanding his world and his values.

Stars Shining in the Dark

When you think about experiences of alienation or discrimination, it is easy to make the seemingly wise choice not to address these issues at all. People often approach this issue by saying: "As parents and teachers, what can we do when facing such a widespread phenomenon? Time will do its part. Once marriages from different communities were rare, but today there is hardly a family that has not been blessed with another ethnicity joining through marriage. Here, too, we already have a first officer from the newly arrived Bnei Menashe tribe of India, an Ethiopian judge, and a well-respected army pilot from Ofakim (a town on the socioeconomic periphery)."

These examples are generally accompanied by the names of celebrities who broke the glass ceiling. While it is important to mention such examples, it is more important to remember that 'stars only shine at night.' They help us to navigate and orient ourselves, but if we feel the need to point to one star, it means it is mostly dark and steps need to be taken to change this.

Members of the educational community's legal team have a different response to racism: "Let's not talk about the ethnic issue," they say, hoping to keep the problems underground. But reality shows us that this issue makes itself known whether we talk of it or not.

At a recent demonstration against racism in front of the central police headquarters in Jerusalem, a young Israeli man of Ethiopian origin arrived with a white shirt printed in black: *Racism — dare to talk about it*. We educators need to dare to talk about the existence of social gaps, prejudices and other forms of racism in society. Talk must be backed up by action. And of course, we need to remember that not every questionable statement is an expression of racism.

Strengthening Belonging in an Alienated Reality

At the beginning of this book, we noted the belief that: "Education leads society and does not lag behind it." Educators must lead society to a place in which every citizen can contribute to the common fabric of life without obscuring his or her identity.

In order to achieve this, we will return to the three basic principles of the Village Way, which relate to the educational community as a whole village, to the educator as a supportive adult, and to the child as a seeker of meaning.

1.   The Whole Village: A Heterogeneous Educational Community as an Island of Stability

Educational communities should be islands of sanity and stability for our youth. Every teen can feel a sense of healing through belonging to an educational community. This is a complex process, but experience proves that it is possible. The blessing of diversity enables us to give all members of the community a fuller, more stable, and more constructive human experience. Homogeneous educational communities lack this resource because the students do not really get the chance to meet 'the other.' To maximize the benefits of diversity, educational staff should conduct activities that will enable the students (and staff) to internalize the power of creating varied connections. We want to teach students to see diversity as a blessing and as an advantage that society has to offer.

2.   Supportive Adult who Fosters Belonging

Every mentor in an educational community should remember that to educate is to foster a sense of belonging. A child who feels that his cultural background is illegitimate will not feel that he belongs. Every supportive adult on the educational team should recognize that the rainbow of colors and cultures that make up society is a national, educational, and moral resource. This is a major educational advantage for the educator, the community, and all of society.

3.   Child Searches for Meaning and Belonging

The student seeking meaning may find it when he expresses his empowered self to the community. Thus, alongside meaning, the young person develops a sense of belonging to the community with—and thanks to—recognition of his identity and cultural heritage.

There are schools which place immigrant students as well as those from certain socioeconomic backgrounds, national identities, and religious or ethnic groups into one group (separate from other students) to offer them extra help. The students are then starting from a place that highlights their supposed disadvantage, which can lead to feelings of alienation. To fit them all into one classroom, the well-intentioned educational staff may be mostly involved with how to fill in missing knowledge and skills. In such a case, the students are perceived by the educators primarily as lacking, a message that is ultimately understood by their peers, as well.

To ensure that the student feels he belongs, he cannot be just a vessel for knowledge. We need to ask ourselves: What can we learn from him? What does he have to share and how do we allow him to express it in front of the whole community? The effort to include different students in community life should be the result of our desire to improve the educational community, not just to help them adjust. Our meetings with students are encounters between individuals. If we do not come ready to accept this and change prejudices that are hidden within us, we may be able to impart knowledge, but we will not succeed in educating.

Mixed Groups: *Treasure or Trouble?*

In most societies there are a wide range of communities and cultures. Often, in a single educational community, there will be adolescents from different cultural backgrounds with conflicting values and various outlooks, who each possess different levels of language proficiency. With this blessed diversity, the educator needs to prepare students for national tests, lead an annual class trip and go to *Tikkun Olam* activities. What happens to teens who do not feel safe in such an environment and dare not speak Hebrew in the presence of native-born Israelis? What about a student who is entitled to a national exam adapted for immigrants, but cannot utilize this benefit because he is in an integrated class? Should we prioritize immediate integration when not everyone is ready for it? In my experience, there are students who will never feel ready and never feel they belong, so they stop trying to integrate. Therefore, the position of those who support integration is to proceed, nonetheless. Having said that, while we work towards integrated groups, we need not do this at all costs. Sometimes it is correct to allow, or even recommend, separation for different communities who may learn best together.

Conditions for Isolating Groups with Unique Cultural Characteristics:

- **Focused Needs:** Before you separate a group, you need to know why you are doing it and what their unique needs are. Needs can be existential, emotional, or ethical.
- **Temporary:** The goal is integration. Therefore, a separate group needs to be defined as temporary, as a reinforcement step towards integration. Just as a fetus develops in her mother's womb, and just as a child at the beginning of her life establishes his habits while experimenting in the bosom of his family, we should enable a safe

environment for the adolescent going through difficult transitions. This temporary nature has two characteristics. First, the length of time that a separate group will exist; for example, holding a separate class for new immigrants the first year or two after arrival. Secondly, built into the schedule on a daily or weekly basis should be an unmediated encounter with students from other groups.

- **Voluntary:** Belonging to a separate group should come with the consent of the participants, with the understanding that this step is the right one for them. For the most part, it is not really possible to let each individual child make solely independent choices in the educational community, but it is still the duty of the educator to present him with the rationale for decisions, such as the choice to have him study in a special class. If he is not convinced that this is the best course of action, he should be given a short trial period in the regular group, and then educators can try again to convince him. If they are not successful, he should be left in the regular group, even if it is against the professional opinion, so as not to exacerbate his feelings of alienation or unworthiness. Even if all these conditions exist and indeed the groups are separated, one must bear in mind the problems associated with the separation. Working with separate groups is usually so convenient that you can get used to this comfort. You may then find reasons, and even excuses, why you should continue to do so, without really needing to.

Our experience shows that a young person who has experienced the process of strengthening his identity and sense of belonging in a separate environment for a limited period of time may later integrate and contribute his share to Israeli society as an equal—and sometimes as the first among equals.

We have become familiar with the 'past-future timeline.' We have seen how the daily educational process can harness the past and the present and create meaningful 'anchors' for youth. This helps them to form their own identities, to grow from strong roots so that their future shines bright with hope. The vulnerability of the teenage years requires youth to put down 'anchors in the past and future.'

This is done in three steps:

- Step One: **Connecting to the past and the future**—familiarizing ourselves with the student's perceptions of the past and his or her personal, communal, and cultural life story, as well as the personal future toward which he or she aspires.
- Step Two: Helping with **understanding the narrative and the existing points of view** of the past and of the future that awaits.
- Step Three: **Identifying Anchors in the Past and in the Future:** We illuminate the points of light and strength in the story of a student's past and locate insights about his or her capabilities and strengths. We then complete the narrative by presenting a system of expectations for the personal and collective future, as well as consistent educational activity that reflects on and guides toward these anchors.

Core Principles of the Timeline: *Past*

Know where you came from *and where you are going*

Anchors in the Past

Empowering connection to the personal past and one's cultural community provides teenagers with self-worth and self-respect.

"Know where you came from" from *Pirkei Avot* [Ethics of our Fathers] 3:1[17] asks us to get to know and connect with the past.

Educators need to create opportunities for the students:
- To become familiar with their past
- To recognize parts of their past
- To choose points of strength
- To connect to points of strength
- To connect the points to a narrative that allows them to tell their personal story from a perspective that promotes growth

Three Elements of Anchors in the Past:
- **Personal Past:** Empowering the personal-familial past
- **Communal-National Past:** Strengthening the collective past, the cultural heritage of the community, the people and the society that surrounds us
- **One Multifaceted Culture:** Encouraging respect, tolerance and dialogue between different cultures

---

17 *Mishna Yomit*, Translated by Dr. Joshua Kulp in Sefaria.com

Core Principles of the Timeline: *Future*

Know where you come from and **where you are going**

Anchors in the Future

"It is a peculiarity of Man that he can only live by looking into the future."
—Viktor Frankl[18]

A broad, positive and organized picture of the future impacts actions in the present.

In working toward a positive future, educators need to address the following student fears:

- The fear of being alone
- The fear of the unknown
- The fear of lacking skills to deal with life's challenges

The educational community should continue to support its graduates.

The educators need to invest in imparting life skills as they present a wide array of future life options, all the while guiding the students to create personalized images of the future.

Three Elements of Anchors in the Future:

- **Image of the Future:** A picture of the future created by offering students a broad range of future opportunities and possibilities; using graduates as part of the educational process as examples or role models
- **"With you all the way":** Offering ongoing support to graduates and making this known among current students
- **Life Skills:** Imparting tools, skills and training for the future

18 Frankl, *Man's Search for Meaning: An Introduction to Logotherapy*

CHAPTER 2

From Earth to Sky: *Creating Meaning in the Educational Space*

Formative Design

Environment influences the educational process. A person's environment, like how they dress, suggests something about the person and has an effect on him. Just as a messy room with dirty clothes on the floor, can reflect something about an individual, so too can faded, dated bulletin boards in a school hallway send the message that we don't respect ourselves or our students. If we seek to educate with human dignity, we should ensure that the educational environments express that concept, along with other values.

Neat rooms, well-maintained, clean and safe spaces and updated bulletin boards—all of these convey the message that we respect ourselves, our students and the work of education. The environment is a significant factor that sends a message and sets an example.

Parallel to our concept of a 'timeline,' the Village Way uses the term **spaceline** to refer to the principles and values that we wish to instill as well as the different educational environments in which we work. Within the 'spaceline,' the **earth** refers to the field on which the educational community's daily life takes place and the **sky** is our word for the moral underpinning that the educational community chooses, expressed in its higher principles.

In education, as in life, there is a gap between the idealistic reality to which we aspire and what occurs on the ground. This tension between the real (the 'earth') and the ideal (the 'sky') raises many questions regarding courses of action within education. How do we relate to our students' lived life? Should education aspire to change the actual situation in favor of the ideal picture—and if so, how?

As educators and as parents, we are familiar with the confusion that results from the discrepancy between what we believe and what actually occurs. The fundamental dilemma is always present: Do I insist on what I believe is right or do I bend to the existing reality? The case of smoking in educational spaces is just one example in which these kinds of deliberations arise.

Sky without Smoke

At the youth village, we specified that there was to be no smoking. This was chosen by our community to honor the value of staying healthy and the need to preserve the environment. This was an idealistic statement, a reality that we were striving toward, part of the 'sky' of our community. However, in practice, we saw the distance between what we believed and the actual reality. We found countless cigarette butts on the ground, and it was clear that not only were there people smoking, but also littering. This was putting us in danger of burning the whole place down, since we are located next to a forest. Our 'earth,' or environment, was acting in opposition to our 'sky,' our moral and educational North Star.

How were we to deal with this discrepancy? It was obvious there were smokers in our community—students, guests and educators. Since we had declared that the environment was to be smoke-free, we had not put ashtrays anywhere or designated smoking areas; and so, every slightly secluded place became a smoking area, and every patch of ground became an ashtray. We met to decide how to deal with this discrepancy. We knew we would educate the community and hold lessons around the issue of smoking and the value of preserving our health, but we also knew that the educational process would be long and winding; and in the meantime, the fact was that there were smokers.

Some of us, including me, were opposed to burying our heads in the sand. Out of responsibility to the whole environment, I felt it was important that together with educational activities on the topic, we designate areas intended for smoking, or at the very least, put out ashtrays. There were those who argued strongly that if we put out ashtrays, we would be conveying contradictory messages. To express this using the Village Way terms: We could not declare our 'sky' free of smoke and still allow for smoking on 'earth.'

After a long deliberation, it was decided at last— against the wishes of some— to put out ashtrays with a small sign next to each that said, "If you have chosen to smoke, which is discouraged, please put out your cigarette here so it won't start a forest fire."

This was not an example of community hypocrisy. The phrase "smoke-free village" reflected our aspiration toward a different reality, and the fact that there were smokers did not contradict the vision. We can say that we do not allow smoking, but we cannot ignore that the phenomenon exists.

This is an example of the kind of complex set of circumstances that young or overworked educational teams tend to see in black and white and may have difficulty handling. It is extremely important to work with staff to confront complex situations so that we can teach students about the tension between existing reality and the aspiration toward a better one. Our community's stance on smoking reflected the tension between our ability to fight the phenomenon and our choice to invest the energy in an educational campaign aimed at teaching students to respect themselves and maintain their health. Of course, such campaigns influence some more than others.

At a different high school, they may have decided to show zero tolerance for every act of smoking, and of course, not to designate smoking areas. Educational communities that allow smoking often feel a sense of shame. As an educator, administrator and parent, I need to ask myself what educational messages my students get from permission to smoke. What kind of message is sent when there are cigarette butts in an ashtray or on the ground? Where do I draw the line and where do I bury my head in the sand? Designating a smoking area without presenting the value behind not smoking is problematic, just as an all-out war on those who violate the rule without any thought to the individual's struggle with the urge to smoke is also problematic. As educators who seek to be supportive and have an impact, we need to be aware of the influence of our environment on education and the individual.

> *"A shelf can complement the bulletin board. We have none in the Children's Home as yet, but we feel the need of it. On the shelf: a dictionary, a collection of proverbs, an encyclopedia, description and plan of the city, anthologies, a calendar, a book of games and amusements. Let there be a place on the shelf for notebooks in which the children may write odds and ends. One scribbles catchy songs, another jokes, a third puzzles, a fourth accounts of his dreams... The reports of monitors may be kept here together with diaries. The teacher's diary, too. Not every diary needs to be kept under lock and key. It seems to me that one to which the teacher confides his disappointments, difficulties, mistakes, items gratifying and joyful, as well as painful, may be of considerable impact."* [19]
>
> —Janusz Korczak, Polish-Jewish educator

Earth

Truth Grows from the Earth

The ethical ideal that guides the community and its educators, which in the Village Way we call the 'sky,' then transforms into daily activity, or the 'earth.' Seen together, this is what we call the 'spaceline' of a community, which serves as its foundation. This movement is constant. We are located on a certain place on this axis and move along it mindfully, just as drivers

---

19   Janusz Korzczak. "The Shelf," *The Selected Works of Janusz Korczak*, (Washington, D.C.: The National Science Foundation, 1967)

use a GPS to navigate. We pay attention to the route itself, to its beautiful landscapes and the occasional obstacles we encounter as well as the crossroads and turns. We stay on course toward the destination that we wish to reach, while being mindful of the need to occasionally adjust course.

The unique compass of the 'spaceline' allows us to connect between the sublime heavenly direction, the 'sky,' which is beyond the everyday reality, and the many varied paths that compose the 'earth,' the educational environment that the 'sky' produces. The verse "Truth springs up from the earth; justice looks down from heaven" (Psalms 85:12)[20] can be interpreted in multiple ways, referencing the connection between the ideal and the real, between 'sky' and 'earth.' The way in which we live our lives on the ground, the 'earth,' has the power to foster an ethical society. To educate toward ethical truth and to make it flourish, we need to adapt it to the 'earth.' Truth springs from the 'earth,' from our environment and day-to-day reality.

An educational community that works with the Village Way concept of the 'spaceline' creates an authentic connection between the human need to find meaning on the one hand, and the everyday reality on the other. It offers educators, parents, and the entire community a tool to understand the current educational situation and to navigate toward growth and progress:

- **Stage 1: Mapping out the Educational Space.** In this stage, we identify our 'spaceline' as it currently exists. We define the community's core values, vision and educational principles. Then we look at the physical space—our 'earth'—and consider what it conveys. What values are the students absorbing and internalizing through the physical space? How does the public space look—the classrooms, activity spaces and the entrance to the school? Are there inspiring pictures and quotes from important historical or contemporary figures in the hallways and classrooms?

- **Stage 2: Confrontation Between Earth and Sky**: At this stage, we bring together the truth reflected in our physical space (earth) and our educational values (sky). We place them opposite one another and analyze whether they agree. Does the environment convey values that contrast with the spirit of the place, like graffiti and cigarette butts littering the floor of a place of learning? If not, does the environment serve the place's values? What do we learn from the discrepancy between what we believe and what actually happens? For example, if we wish our teenagers to be book lovers, have we placed the library in a central location? Are there bookshelves in the classrooms and hallways? Should we also put in televisions, and if so, where? In the center of the home or in a corner? Are the values that are important to us expressed in the design of the environment? Do the pictures and quotes in the hallways and classrooms of the school reflect what we believe regarding expressions of diversity and gender? Will pictures of our family decorate the office? At this stage, we are stepping back and considering our place on the 'spaceline.' We are marking the difference between what is desired and our current reality.

- **Stage 3: Taking Action**: During this stage, we translate our principles into practice, so that they reflect our educational 'sky' and meet our 'earth' in an authentic way. This process is expressed through direct action taken in different areas, including the school regulations, *derech eretz*, (Hebrew for manners and considerate behavior), the culture of discourse and interpersonal relationships, and finally, the physical appearance of different spaces.

All of this forms the basis for translating 'sky' to 'earth' and cultivating a meaningful educational environment that influences each person as "the imprint of his native landscape," in the words of Hebrew poet Shaul

Tchernikovsky.[21] It becomes an internal imprint that forges a path. This is carried out simultaneously on three levels: aesthetics, familial atmosphere, and the content/essence.

Aesthetics

The word aesthetics in its contemporary interpretation refers to beauty and its impact on humans. The word is of Greek origin: *aisthēsis*, meaning sensory perception. When we speak of aesthetics in education, we refer to the sensory consciousness of the students and educators and to the way in which the world, and the local community and culture, define beauty, a concept that traditionally includes all that is good, worthy, and moral. In other words, the physical spaces of our 'earth,' through aesthetics, represent the principles of our 'sky.' In each educational community, the aesthetics will be unique and different.

The aesthetic common to all our communities is a clean and dignified living environment. You do not ignore trash in the yard and you certainly don't start a lesson in a filthy classroom. Any educator that comes across trash should pick it up and throw it in the garbage in a natural and easy way. Usually, this act sends a clearer message about the importance of cleanliness than would instructing a student to throw it out.

> *I recall one marathon study session at Yemin Orde Youth Village before the compulsory Bible matriculation exam. Many students showed up, but the classroom was filthy due to a party that had been held there the night before. The immediate options were to ignore the mess and teach for the test, or to start cleaning, using time that should be spent studying. Each choice had its benefits. Studying is important, but so is cleanliness. Respect for my time as an educator, and for the time of every one of the students that showed up, was also a concern. I could go find a cleaner classroom, or I could, as an alternative, consider a complex response to a complex reality.*

---

21   Shaul Tchernichovsky, *HaAdam Eino Elah*, (Berlin), 1924

In this case, unlike in other similar incidents in the past, I chose to overcome my feelings of being a pushover, and I started to clean. There were students who joined me and students who got angry that we were wasting time. I told them that I respected them, and therefore, I was unwilling to teach the lesson in a dirty classroom. "As far as I am concerned, you are people who deserve respect. Even if you are willing to give up this respect, I insist on honoring you with the respect you deserve. We will clean up and then start studying." The more secure I felt in my role as a supportive educational leader, the less I cared about the opinions of others regarding what tasks might be perceived by others as beneath my own dignity.

I know this experience from the other side as well. At the beginning of the year, I came to the high school area and saw a snack wrapper on the ground in the yard. I threw it away in the garbage, and immediately after, I heard one of the older students laughing at me and saying: "There's a trash can over there, and you can go pick up more garbage right here." It was an embarrassing moment. If that had been my only experience with the issue, I would have found it difficult to go into the classroom and clean up before that marathon study session, as I would have felt disrespected. But being a part of a Village in which my colleagues also take part in campus maintenance, I had, over time, also seen many students join in on the cleaning. This is probably what enabled me to act naturally, in a way that did not sacrifice our study time, but neither did it discount the importance of cleanliness in the classroom and respecting the student environment. Above all, it helped me understand that every one of my choices conveyed a message about a value-based decision.

Does Wealth Corrupt or Enable?

As we approach the aesthetic design of our space, we aspire to express our spirit and enable the best possible learning experience. The sensory-aesthetic vision can be expressed in a variety of ways, from sophisticated works of art to cutting-edge technology to a natural connection to the surrounding landscape. There should be a congruence between the essence of the community and its physical spaces. In this way, the physical aspect will deepen a sense of belonging to the community, express its values, and create a warm, dignified and homelike feeling.

Sometimes, we find ourselves wondering how to proceed with design. Such a situation arose when one of the Village Way educational communities won a prize and the proposition was made to invest most of the prize money in physical spaces and equipment. If accepted, the school would undergo a transformation from a place lacking in design and equipment to one full of abundance and progress. The educational staff deliberated about the effect of the physical changes on the psyche of each community member and the spirit of the place. They considered whether, as Israel's former Education Minister Shai Peron once said, "The quality of the pillow determines the quality of the dream,"[22] meaning that in order to enable the students to dream big, the physical environment should express economic and technological abundance. They also considered whether simple conditions were a more suitable platform for education and if opulence could pose a distraction. Proponents for that view cited the Biblical story of Jacob, who fled to Haran and slept on the side of the road with only a rock under his head as a pillow. That simple setup led to Jacob's momentous dream of a ladder connecting earth and heaven with meaning and purpose.

Parents also sometimes confront issues regarding the values we convey to our children, whether we choose to buy them brand name clothing or the newest smartphone. In a world in which, more than ever before, the global culture glorifies consumerism—does wealth and abundance corrupt the human psyche or expand it in a positive fashion? Clearly, there is much room to maneuver between a neglected environment and an ostentatious one. It is perfectly acceptable to create a positive aesthetic environment, even on a small budget. We need to remember that the environment is a resource at our disposal. We have the ability, perhaps even the obligation, to utilize it to shape reality.

Design a Change

An educator seeking to bring about a focused educational impact can look to the various physical spaces to help him generate it. Often, to change something fundamental, it is necessary to just change something simple or structural—and the new pattern leads to substantive change. Even if many of the school buildings are old, and it is difficult to create a pleasant atmosphere of abundance and quality, we can commit to making the best effort with what we have available.

I remember when one of the Village Way educational communities sought to deepen the students' sense of belonging to the school and the community. The general feeling was that the students felt, at best, like guests, and at worst, completely alienated. A profound change was sought. The school staff wanted to enlist the Village Way 'earth' concept, and they asked themselves how the physical spaces would look if the students felt like they belonged. This was a school that was tastefully decorated and did not have old buildings, but the school staff decided to upgrade the campus by reorganizing most spaces and creating dedicated student areas. Formal and informal educational activities for individuals and classes were directed toward this goal. The school also decided to purchase cameras, and students were asked to take photographs over a long period, to present the landscape as they saw it. The photographs placed alongside quotes from the Bible or by important figures chosen by the students were printed, and displayed in various spaces, with the artist's name appearing next to each photograph. Within a short time, students began to walk around proudly, showing each other their pictures. Personal points of view as well as a discussion about the nature of the community were shared;

and it soon became evident that the school's collective sense of family and belonging had deepened.

Safe, Family Atmosphere: *The 'Area Out Back'*

Every place, including educational spaces, has an 'area out back,' and we should get to know it, or at least, recognize its existence. The area out back—in both the physical and symbolic senses—has an important role in a person's growth and education. This is where significant processes of rebellion, self-expression, interpersonal interactions, and "positive" and "negative" behaviors all come together. Each educational community relates to its own version of such a space, strengthening aspects of the student experience that more formal spaces rarely allow. What are the teens that go to the area out back to have a deep conversation or to drink and fool around telling us?

There are a few possibilities:

- We are aware of the rules and values, both the 'sky' and 'earth' behaviors expected of us.
- We respect the leadership or are afraid of their response, and therefore, we are not doing these things out in the open.
- We, like every normative teenager, want a place of our own where we determine the rules.

To a certain extent, parents and educators find it more convenient to avoid dealing with certain phenomena in a direct way. In this way, the 'area out back' preserves our sanity as well.

Often, adults struggle against this permissive space, but we need to understand that the problems will not disappear when it is shut down. If we close the 'area out back,' it could easily turn into the frontlines of the educational community. When dealing with teens at home, for example, we can disallow an activity, only to find our youngsters returning home smelling of alcohol or cigarettes, or alternately, smelling of strong perfume to disguise something.

As the parents of an adolescent son, my wife and I have dealt with this. Our teenage son went to a community youth hangout place that, while public, felt to us like an 'area out back.' He realized this did not match the ethical behavior we expected of him, but he wanted to taste the forbidden fruit and continue to hang out there. As parents, we realized that if we had succeeded at conveying an ethical message, while accepting that a certain amount of rebellion is a part of growing up, that is enough. We cannot agree with the negative behavior and should insist on the boundary; but will we be able to completely stop a teen from going to the 'area out back?' Probably not.

Sometimes, however, we may elect to take a space that functions in this way and turn it into a decent place. In cases like this, we know that the area does not completely disappear, but merely changes location. This is what Dr. Chaim Peri did as Director of Yemin Orde Youth Village when he succeeded in turning one 'area out back' from a place of mischief to the display window for the whole community.

The synagogue at Yemin Orde Youth Village has always been the most impressive building on the campus. It was built on the side of the mountain, creating a large hidden space in the back supported by pillars. That little area was known to be a shady place on hot sunny days, as well as a comfortable shelter from the rain, with a view of the sea, and most importantly—it was hidden from the watchful eyes of the adults. And so, an 'area out back' was created in the heart of the Village, right under our eyes. In response, we increased the adult presence in the area, and later, we fenced off the area and put up a gate with a lock, turning the space into a furniture storage area.

However, we soon discovered that one of the bars of the gate had been removed and kids had gone in and met up there—not to study for exams. Even though this space was located below the synagogue, the goings on there were far from holy. All protective and preventative measures failed in dealing with this area, until we decided that instead of fighting a war on a dark space, we would introduce a new light. We renovated the space into a meeting room. Soon, the space became a center of campus activity frequented by community members and visitors. This allowed most students who had not frequented the area when it was abandoned, as well as those who had used the place to feel respected.

And the 'area out back?' It found a new home... Inspired by the previous success, the educational community chose to take the senior students to the new 'area out back' and ask them what they suggested be done to change it. After a long process, an idea was put forth to create a memorial to two graduates from the class who had died in violent incidents outside of the village. The decision was made to turn a large part of the space into a lookout point in memory of these graduates, a place dedicated to the sanctity of life and to eradicating violence. It was to include a memorial monument and a poem about the beauty and sanctity of life. The class decided the monument be made with transparent materials to emphasize that violent acts are often ignored although the victims are crying out to be seen; and also to underscore that transparency is the key to solving the problem. In addition to the monument, the lookout point was to serve as the location where a community-wide process for mediating disputes in cases of violence would take place. The space has evolved from a dark, unpleasant one into a place from which you can see the horizon in two ways: the spectacular physical horizon of Mount Carmel down to the Mediterranean Sea and the figurative horizon, in which there is unity, fraternity, and sanctity of life.

A Sense of Security

When there are problems, an educational community's responsibility to protect their students can lead to protective measures, such as installing locks, fences, or cameras. Sometimes, it is unclear whether these protective security measures undermine a community's sense of security and family by breeching privacy, or whether the assurance of personal and communal security increases the students' sense of belonging and family.

> *At one Village Way educational community located in the center of Israel, a serious wave of theft began after students and staff returned from Passover vacation. As a result, some of the parents and teachers called for security cameras to be installed. The principal decided to have an in-depth discussion about the issue. Parents, educators, and students were involved in this discussion, which took place over the course of a whole day. Together they deliberated the ethical dilemmas and practical solutions that would maintain a sense of community and safety. Afterward, everyone agreed that the discourse itself, and the shared experience of thinking through the topic, reinforced the message that theirs was a community of meaning, committed to the protection of its members.*

It is important to remember that fences and cameras are not the point. Though technological measures do not compromise the spirit of the community, neither do they guarantee security. It is possible that at one school, the use of cameras might reduce the human presence in certain places, thereby diminishing the familial atmosphere. At another school fully equipped with cameras, the sense of community may still be evident due to the administration ensuring that students understand the goal is to protect them, and not be protected from them.

Even after we decide if, and where, to place the cameras, we then need to think about where to install the split screen that displays the recorded images. Do you display the screen to anyone who enters the main office, 'Big Brother' style, or locate it in a place hidden from plain sight, to be checked only when an event occurs that requires it? Cameras do not replace human presence, nor do they preclude the need for an investigative process in which the students are asked about a problematic incident. Nonetheless, cameras may reduce conflict surrounding the facts and allow for greater focus on a proactive solution.

It is important to remember that even if there is meaningful dialogue before fences or cameras are installed, new students join each year. It is, therefore, necessary to have the same discussion with the new students, and not just limit such a discussion to a one-time event. It is worthwhile to choose a fixed date during the year on which the topic is addressed, and not allow a wave of thefts to determine the community agenda.

A Room of One's Own

Educational communities can create a warm, inviting space that strengthens the sense of belonging among the students, a kind of students' lounge designed for breaks in the schedule. One community I know of established a girls' space, and another set up a lounge with hot drinks under the auspices of the student council. The main thing is to encourage the sense among the teens that this is a space that belongs to them.

In our experience, a youth village becomes the central space in the life of students. Since the students live there, a sense of family is necessary. As educators, we often juggle organizational realities with emotional considerations that help convey a sense of family—as in the case of Tanya.

For some youth, like Tanya, a youth village is their only home in Israel. To ensure her sense of home over the many years she lived with us from a young age, we had been careful not to move her from the room where she lived with her friends. When she reached the 10th grade, we had no choice but to move her from this room, due to a safety issue. We sat down to talk with Tanya and her roommates, and they expressed tremendous resistance to any change because they said this physical space was an emotionally significant homelike anchor in their lives. As far as we administrators were concerned, we had exhausted all other options—logistically, there was simply no way to keep Tanya and her roommates in that room. And so, as the head of informal education, I had to give instructions that the students leave their room—but they soon let us know there was no way they were going to move!

The conversation between us focused on belonging and home. At first, Tanya was angry and said that we could not remove her from her home and that if we did, we would be on her blacklist. She explained that she divides the world into "people I love and people I hate." Unfortunately, she told us the list of people she hated was much longer. "If you move me out of the room, you will be on the list of people I hate," she shouted. We went back to the office to try to think of other solutions, but we failed. We tried to work with her to find a way to bring the same warm, homey feeling into the new room. After a long and complex process, Tanya and her friends moved to their new room. It took time for the anger to subside, but eventually, Tanya made peace with the move. The conversation between us—though not easy, to say the least—conveyed that we understood and respected her, and especially, that the community was committed to functioning as a substitute home in the broadest sense. Nonetheless, the experience highlighted the fact that, despite all efforts, the Village was not really a home, just the closest thing to it.

There is an innate tension between the needs and desires of the students and the constraints of the system. Sometimes, it is necessary to bend the system's inherent red lines, and sometimes, to maintain them. But we should always consider the implications for the students. In a case like Tanya's, we would never lie and say that we were moving her to a new room to improve her view and that we are unconcerned with her reaction.

Let us pause for a moment to think about Tanya's threat: "If you move me out of the room, you will be on the list of people I hate." That sentence can either draw in the adult or distance them. With that statement, Tanya was playing on our fears of being inconsiderate adults who do not understand the needs of young people. Surely, we want to be on the list of people she loves. She is using manipulation that indicates she sees the world in black and white. She needs the adults in her life to prove to her that there is more to life than this, that there is a rather wide gray area, that people on the hated list may actually love her or at least care about her. Such a response from the adults in her life blurs the edges, enabling her to experience vulnerability as well as trust.

I remember an extreme case of theft at Yemin Orde, in which the staff deliberated as a group whether to search students' bags. There was ambiguity surrounding the legality of such a search. We knew that searching would probably help identify the thief but would also create a very unpleasant feeling among the students and educators, precisely because the educational community is meant to be a safe, familial atmosphere. Such a conundrum is familiar to parents as well as educators. As parents, we need to decide what has greater priority—protecting our children's safety or protecting their privacy. Simple questions induce honest bewilderment regarding how to parent: Should you go into your child's computer and check what websites he is visiting or respect their privacy? Should you find out exactly where they are hanging out and with whom? Often, despite such questions, we decide that it is our duty to protect our children and teens, and to intrude into their lives.

In the context of an educational community, it is sometimes better that the supportive adults take care of the 'policing' task, which can be embarrassing for youth, instead of leaving it to a security professional who does not necessarily care about the educational process. A security guard may be asked to deal with certain disciplinary actions, but it is necessary to mediate between him and the students, to explain to the young people why an external person was chosen and to request their cooperation. It is important to soften these unilateral situations.

The tension between familial atmosphere and community safety comes up in various ways. For example, we may ask whether, in our effort to create a familial atmosphere, we should allow students access to all areas within the community—including the teachers' rooms—or whether there is a need for basic boundaries? These decisions also depend on the spirit of the place, its values and rules. It is important to remember that the space itself conveys meaningful messages and values.

Daily life delineated by routines also affects the community's sense of family and security. School bells, ceremonies, and the way personal conversations take place between adults and teenagers express the nature of a place. On an emotional level, boundaries create a sense of security and order for the student, a stable world to be experienced and even rebelled against as part of adolescence. Many times, it is the permanent surroundings and the daily routine that create stable ground for the student, the 'earth' on which he or she can stand and grow.

This is an example of the way in which the 'spaceline' influences a person's soul— organizing the educational space within structures that encourage security, order and emotional resilience. Many children and teenagers need a clear space defined by a fixed routine, a schedule and a clear framework. For some, this is not a technical issue, but an emotional framework that creates a sense of calm and provides energy for development.

Content and Essence
The Village Way concept of 'earth' includes the formal and informal educational routine, the schedule, physical spaces and the entire way of life. In an educational context, 'earth' expresses content and meaning, which joins with the spirit, values and essence, indicated by the 'sky.'

Speaking to Trees and Stones
As soon as one enters a school, a subliminal message to the students and staff emerges, but the message does not always represent what the educational community most wishes to instill. The pictures, bulletin boards, and announcements show visitors who the role models are as well as something about the ethical-educational language spoken there. An empty wall is essentially blank media, conveying a message through

absence and deeply influencing the spirit of the place. Bulletin boards play an important role and they are 'active partners' in the educational process. In a world flooded with advertising agencies selling products in overt and covert ways, we as educators need to 'sell' values with all the resources at our disposal. We cannot join the brainwashing competition, but we cannot stay out of the game. We need to stay relevant.

Pine trees, which are scattered throughout Israel, help us remember this point. Such trees often grow in the yards of many Israeli schools. Exposed stone walls are also often found in educational spaces. This can remind us of the frustrating experience of speaking when no one is listening, or to use a Hebrew phrase: "talking to the trees and the stones." As a response to this feeling, we seek to create an alternative: "Trees and stones, talk to me!" an ongoing interactive dialogue. In this way, pine trees, native to Eastern Europe and present in Israel as well, have taken on a special significance for us. Israeli poet Leah Goldberg saw pine trees as a sign of the connection between her two homelands: the Jewish homeland of Israel and her personal homeland in Lithuania. Pines helped her feel less out of place, but also signified a new beginning informed by her past.

As she wrote:

"With you I was transplanted twice,
With you, pine trees, I grew –
Roots in two disparate landscapes."[23]

In schools in Israel, students learn that many Israelis originally emigrated from other parts of the globe, just like Goldberg. With the help of the pines on the Yemin Orde campus, we can convey the importance of recognizing the longing for one's birthplace alongside one's sense of connection to Israel. Our students are told that they do not have to uproot themselves, that both of their homelands are important and good. We

---

23 Leah Goldberg. "Pine [*Oren*]," in *Morning Lightning*, [*Barak Ba-Boker*] (Sifriat Poalim, 1955)

teach the Goldberg poem and hang it next to a pine tree. The tree thus becomes an active partner in the educational process and continues to convey a message every time the students walk past.

A strong, rooted identity cannot be built only on the cognitive-content level, but it does not just rely on feelings. Identity requires the creation of broad contexts of meaning and identification based on a comprehensive sense of knowledge. Content, aside from being central to the formal and informal learning spaces, needs to be reflected in other spaces within the educational 'earth.'

In most educational communities that use the Village Way methods, we see effective use of bulletin boards, designed to enhance the collective experience. When one of our groups begins a major volunteer activity, information on the bulletin board enhances the experience and informs all members of the community, creating a sense of partnership. Bulletin boards are also used to highlight outstanding students and current affairs in the community, in Israel and around the world. Using a bulletin board just as a simple message board is a missed opportunity given the educational potential embodied within it. We use the bulletin board as an active resource to highlight success stories and heroism. For example, to mark the Nobel Prize ceremony, you might display pictures of the winners with the type of prize they won, and then add a small mirror and the words: "This place is reserved for you." The same can be done during the Olympic Games within a display of medal winners. The mirror and the inscription continue to be effective even when no adults are in the vicinity since they convey the message: "We believe and trust in you. You can do it. Keep dreaming and striving."

"Truth" sprouts from the 'earth,' expressed in aesthetics, a familial atmosphere and essential content. This helps us relate to the planning, building and ongoing design of the educational space. The physical space influences reality. It conveys the rules, atmosphere and values of the place. A person senses what is permitted and what is forbidden, as well as noting the essence—the *emet*, truth—of the place.

The Broken Windows Theory

In a 1982 article about crime in *The Atlantic Monthly*[24], James Q. Wilson and George L. Kelling presented the broken windows theory, which examined how people behave when they enter a space. An experiment was conducted in which a window in a building in New York City was purposefully broken, and later that same night, those conducting the experiment found that several additional windows had been broken by people unrelated to the study. The study concluded that a broken window conveys neglect, which leads to further neglect and a rise in crime. The experiment was expanded in various ways, and eventually, the researchers came to the conclusion that when a person sees a broken window, he gets the sense that there are no clear rules or that the codes of conduct encourage negative behavior, that disrespect and crime are preferable to preserving the environment.

In keeping with the broken windows theory, human behavior is such that if you enter a clean, organized place you will conclude that it is a place of law and order. Adapting this theory from criminology to the field of education, we can learn about the nature of humans and the 'earth'—about our physical spaces and their influence on us. Our values sprout from the 'earth.' The physical environment and our daily life convey the deepest meaning.

What About Vandalism?

We conclude from the broken windows theory that an immediate response to vandalism is necessary—first to restore the area to its former state as soon as possible, and then, to begin the educational-disciplinary process. Given that one's environment seems to impact on the choice to vandalize, we may wish to refrain from dealing directly with those responsible—*but we should not do this*. We ought to respect all those who did not vandalize and prevent them from being dragged down too.

---

24 George L. Kelling and James Q. Wilson, "Broken Windows: The Police and Neighborhood Safety," *The Atlantic Monthly*. Mar. 1982; 249(3):29–38.

On one visit to a Village Way community, I went into the bathroom and saw, on the door, the sentence: "[name of the community] is the best school in the country." It amused me because I had gotten used to far less positive things written on bathroom doors, so I took a picture of it. I told one of the staff members how flattering it was that a student was writing about the school when he was alone, but I added that it would be best to clean it off soon, as it would invite other comments, and there would probably be those who would not agree with the original writer's assessment of the school. Two weeks later, when I returned to the same place, I hurried to the bathroom and discovered that the sentence had not been erased and that insults and curses of various kinds had been added.

Another example, this one a proper encounter with vandalism:

In one of the Village Way schools, the administrators found that every year they were spending tens of thousands of shekels to repair damages created by student vandalism. One year, at the beginning of the year, the principal divided this annual amount into the number of classrooms and divided the public space between them. He announced that each class would receive NIS 8,000 for a fun activity that would take place at the end of the year. Any class that remained orderly and undamaged would get an additional NIS 2,000 at the end of the year, but a damaged classroom would have to use the money allocated to repair the damage.

We tend to believe that vandalism or property damage occurs in a place where people feel a lack of belonging and caring. This is sometimes true, but not always. Sometimes, vandalism occurs precisely because of a sense of ownership, in which teenagers feel: "We can do with it as we like!" But, regardless of the cause, we need to treat any form of vandalism in the same way: First, we clean and refurbish, and only then, we turn to the educational process. The 'preemptive strike' against vandalism lies in making our youth partners in the design, construction, cleaning and maintenance of their space, and allowing them to work alongside the maintenance staff and the administration to develop a sense of responsibility for the place. It is important for them to understand that we care about the internal consequences of vandalism, the negativity that it leaves within them, and not just the item that was destroyed. We have also realized that the nicer the bathrooms are in their design, the lower the levels of graffiti and vandalism. Respect breeds respect.

A Sky Above Me and Within Me

"Turning around
It does not mean to be free
There is a sky above me
There is a sky within me
Ready for everything
Not afraid until I feel there is a sky
Within me
There is within me sky, and above me "

—Aviv Geffen and Eviatar Banai[25]

The 'Sky' in Adolescent Identity

The 'sky' is the Village Way word to express the meaning in each of our lives. Our basic assumption about human nature is that a valuable life is not created alone. To develop fully, it needs to be connected to a broader significance that goes beyond its immediate existence. Ideals, values, and belonging to a community are all necessary for a person to lead a life of meaning. It is the role of the educator to activate these subtle dimensions by connecting them to the cultural and social pulse of the educational community. This connection nurtures the physiological and emotional needs of adolescence.

25 "There's Sky Above Me," (Hed Arzi Music, 2012)

For example, according to educational philosopher Kieran Egan, the age of adolescence—ages 14 to 20—is the time at which a person is in the philosophical stage.[26] During this stage, young people develop thinking that enables the connection of various details into one larger, overarching picture. Students perceive themselves as part of the world and wish to understand the rules that exist in it. According to Egan, this aspiration is essentially narcissistic because the young people tend to view the world as a mirror. By understanding the legalities and ideologies that underlie their world, they develop their identity within it.

We can all agree on a person's need for meaning, and that adolescence is the appropriate age for laying the proper foundation for this. The question is: how to affix the 'sky' in the hearts of adolescents? Is it even possible? Eviatar Banai and Aviv Gefen sing: "There is a sky inside me and above me." Even if we know that there is a sky above us, how do we integrate it within us and ourselves within it?

Like the heavens themselves, the concept of 'sky' is elusive and challenging to define. Perhaps we should begin with the importance of the principle that every person, every family, and every educational community should have a 'sky,' and that each community defines this concept in its own way.

The 'Sky' as Fundamental Values

We express the 'sky' through our fundamental values, from which our conduct, routine, and rules derive. A growing adolescent in a normative home absorbs values throughout the course of his daily life. He will see how his parents behave when a beggar comes to the door. He will hear his parents' phone calls. In Israel, he will feel the change when his father disappears for military reserve duty. He will attend traditional ceremonies, sit at a holiday meal and be exposed to mutual care in his community and within his family. Gradually, a selection of values will form, which might include the importance of giving,

---

26   Kieran Egan, *Individual Development and the Curriculum*, 1986

accepting the 'other,' family, honesty, patriotism, fear of God, love of books and more. When the time comes, he will consciously decide which values to adopt and which to leave behind. Over the course of his life, he will be exposed to other people and events that represent different or conflicting values, and these others will cause him to reexamine his values and decide whether to update, renew, or add to them.

This process is different for young people who come of age in a collective setting. In an educational community there are numerous educators who expose the adolescents to various values, and this process may also overwhelm him. Such a young person lacks the safety of a central axis of shared fundamental values enjoyed by a child with involved parents. In a place that has arbitrary rules to enable functioning but lacks agreed-upon values, it will be most difficult to help the adolescent find meaning and maintain an optimal educational process. Instead of educating, we might use the word 'training' to describe that kind of situation. Such surroundings focus on changing behavior without the values which encourage the adolescent to shape his own identity.

In every human environment there are agreed-upon values, though they are not usually put in writing. Within educational communities, we should set them down in writing, give them substance and allow the students to examine whether the educators conduct themselves according to these values.

One Friday evening, I received a phone call from my former student Moshe, who had completed his studies the year before and was training for the naval commando unit. The call did not surprise me because we were in close contact. But I was surprised when Moshe asked me to take a photograph of a certain "picture with circles" that hung in his former classroom. I immediately understood what he meant, a poster called "The values to which we are committed." "Why do you need it?" I asked, curiously. He replied: "We had a meeting in our squadron, at which everyone had to present his personal credo. I

remember this page because it made sense to me and I identified with
it." Moshe had always been a very ethical young man who brought
values from his childhood home and added values that he absorbed at
the educational community. He joined the naval commando unit as a
young man who identified with traditional Jewish observance, and
while there, he reassessed his values. It's significant that the poster
he requested didn't just list his own personal values but reflected the
Village Way method of defining one's own belief system based on
shared community values. When as a young adult, he was asked to
share his credo, Moshe returned to the dynamic process of continuously
reshaping his value system, one that he had learned at Yemin Orde.

There is a well-known controversy regarding whether we should seek to inculcate values into young people. To that I say: We believe that values are present throughout the fabric of life. They are not a poster on a wall or a distant destination for which we prepare our students. The values are the 'sky' above us, next to us, and in time, also within us. Instead of education *toward* values, we choose to educate from *within the framework* of values.

The Levels of Moral Judgement

How will the adolescent behave when there is no parent, educator, policeman or anyone else beside him? Psychologist Lawrence Kohlberg's 1975 study[27] on the development of moral judgment points to the existence of six universal developmental stages, which he further divides into three levels. We encourage parents and educators to consider the levels and stages of youth.

Level 1: Compensation: Wages or Punishment

Stage 1: Obedience and Punishment: At this stage, the person focuses on the immediate consequences of his actions alone. The motivation for action

---

27   Lawrence Kohlberg, *The Psychology of Moral Development*, (Harper and Row, 1984)

is either evading punishment or receiving reward. Prevention of punishment and submission to authority are perceived as having merit in themselves.

Stage 2: Reciprocity as a Source of Pleasure: A person is willing to do a good deed for others based on the thought that the beneficiary will return the good deed. If the other person is perceived as the source of a future benefit, then it is worthwhile to try to do something for him. Reciprocity—the key element in thinking at this stage—is always a matter of "one hand washes the other."

Level 2: Social Norms

Stage 3: Conformity to a Group: A person identifies proper behavior with whatever others approve of in his group of affiliation and what may earn him their affections. He asks for confirmation from the other: "You are a good boy." The motive for action is the desire to be loved and accepted.

Stage 4: "Law and Order" as a Foundation for the Existence of Society: The thinking at this stage is aimed at obeying/accepting the authority of rules, legal systems, and social arrangements. Good or fair conduct is judged in accordance with the person's duty to fulfill the laws that ensure social order.

Level 3: Moral Obligation

Stage 5: Social Contract, Human Rights, and Welfare: A person at this stage tends to define a moral act in terms of individual rights in accordance with the general contract of society. He does not ignore legal aspects but emphasizes the possibility of changing laws if the good of society demands it.

Step 6: Universal Ethical Principles: At this stage, humans are guided primarily by their conscience, considering consistent principles such as justice, reciprocity, equality, human rights and respect for the value of life. These principles go beyond any written social document.

Can One Progress in Moral Judgment?

The basic assumption is that the person wants to be moral. The more a person develops in his intellectual understanding, the more his morality develops. Thus, appropriate education may enhance the moral development of young people through cognition. We are not concerned with the "character" or "type" of person, but rather how an individual relates to the ethical issues that he encounters, how he develops ethical awareness. The answer to the question of whether it is possible to aid adolescents in progressing through the levels of moral judgment is yes, absolutely!

According to Kohlberg, progress on the moral justice scale is achieved through learning and practice. The educator should provide opportunities for the teenager to raise questions, disagree, argue, listen to others, examine different points of view and roleplay to examine potential flaws in their thinking.

Kolberg's theory is complex and has its critics. I seek to take from it the simple principle that it is possible to advance in levels of moral judgment and to help others do so. In the world of Jewish morality, it is customary to speak of three steps: the fear of punishment, the fear of sin, and the fear of heaven. The fear of punishment is equivalent to Kohlberg's first level (level of reward), in which we avoid forbidden things out of fear of punishment. It is commonly thought that this level is characteristic of small children, but it can be true of adults, as well. Driving on a highway, we may encounter very ethical adults who speed and slow down at the sight of a police car. On the other hand, adults may follow the rules of the road, not steal and cheat, and yet still disrespect, exploit, and hurt others behind closed doors.

The fear of sin is parallel to Kohlberg's second level, behavior according to social norms, which is often inconsistent in the world of adolescents. The school norms do not necessarily line up with the norms at home and certainly not with those of their peers in the neighborhood. These dichotomies emphasize the importance of working toward cohesion within an educational community.

Fear of heaven, which corresponds to Kohlberg's third level, speaks of values, of the essence of humanity; do I behave according to the values I have chosen? Do I act as someone with a 'sky' above me and inside me?

The fear of heaven will be expressed in the behavior of a graduate when he is alone. Will he participate in hazing that is being done to a young soldier in his platoon, or will he try to prevent it? It depends on the level of moral judgment he has reached. As educators, we should aim to instill moral courage.

The Impact of Educators on Moral Judgment

Our responses as educators have a direct influence on our students' progression in levels of moral judgment. If our response to the negative actions of a 12th grader is identical to the same act by a 9th grader, we are basically saying to him: "We do not expect you to progress. As far as we are concerned, you have remained at the low level of fear of punishment." However, as indicated in the speeding example, moral judgment can be relative. When an educator wants to help a student progress, he or she must choose a proper response to the student's current stage and assist him to progress to the next.

A Cry for HELP

At the beginning of the year, I entered a classroom of 12th graders. The lesson had not yet begun, and only the boys had arrived—and not everyone had noticed that I was in the classroom. Through the large classroom windows, the new girls from the ninth grade appeared. The boys began to talk about the girls' appearance in a disrespectful manner. I could not ignore what I had heard. I shared my feelings with them, that it really bothered me to hear such rude comments. I spoke about the basic morality embodied in the sentence from the Talmud: "That which is hateful unto you, do not do to your neighbor."[28] I asked who had sisters, and how would they like them to be treated. I spoke about holiness and romance, about this miracle we were blessed with by the Creator, or nature, that enables us to create life. How important it is for us to know how to respect our partners

---

28 Tractate Shabbat: 31a

*and treat the act of love with holiness and not just as a physical act
with momentary pleasure!*

*Then I switched to national laws and school rules regarding
consent and relationships of students of different ages. I returned to
the teacher's lounge upset and shared the experience with some of my
colleagues. One of them said: "What are you doing talking to them
about holiness? They are not interested in that. They are teenagers
with raging hormones. It's good that you clarified the law for them."*

My conversation with the seniors was spontaneous, but it was rooted
in an educational model that we at the Village Way have developed
according to the levels of moral judgement. In English, the model can
be represented by the acronym **HELP**,[29] suggestive of the way teenagers
act out, which is really a cry for help. The HELP acronym stands for
Holiness, Ethics, Law, and Partnership. The discourse on holiness speaks
to the high level of values to which Kohlberg referred. We might call
this the level of principles, which appeals to those advanced in moral
judgment and motivated by values. The ethics discourse addresses the level
of social norms and the legal discourse addresses the lowest level, fear of
punishment and expectation of reward. It is important to remember that
educators and youth are partners in this process, rather than adversaries.

Our educational approach needs to include all components of the
model because in each group there are students at different levels. Also,
within each person are expressions of the three levels of judgement, and
we can never be completely certain which channel will reach the teen at
his or her stage of life.

Too often, as educators of young people, we find ourselves aligning
with the legal discourse, and in doing so, lowering the level of discourse
and placing adolescents there. I will continue to insist on discussing the
ideas of romance, holiness, and relationship values with hormone-drenched

---

29   In Hebrew, the model is called KEMACH, the Hebrew word for flour as well as an acronym made
   up of the Hebrew words for holiness (*kdusha*), morality (*musariut*) and law (*chok*).

teenagers because I have not given up my expectations for them. However, I also incorporate additional, possibly more immediately relevant, aspects into the conversation.

The Village Way 'spaceline' emphasizes the creation of a physical environment that enables growth while simultaneously encouraging the adolescent to find meaning. It expresses place, one of the components of a person's identity, and it refers to the place in its totality—the 'earth,' the physical-behavioral essence of the community that shapes the person who grew up in it and that will remain within him throughout his life. The second element in the 'spaceline' is the 'sky,' which symbolizes the higher, moral dimension that charts the mission of the group and the individual.

Core Principles of the 'Spaceline': *Earth*

Earth

"Man is the imprint of his native landscape"
                    —Shaul Tchernichovsky, Israeli poet

The Village Way concept of **earth** means the need to create a stable and aesthetic physical environment, which will convey a sense of both home and the values we want to instill.

The physical dimension is an educational resource that should be used to present the values of the community.

Three Elements of Earth:
- **Aesthetics:** Creating an orderly and beautiful atmosphere
- **Family Atmosphere:** Designing the environment in a way that strengthens the sense of security and conveys familial warmth
- **Content:** Expressing fundamental values through the environment's design

Core Principles of the 'Spaceline': *Sky*

Sky

"Divinity is found in approaching the Other"
—Inspired by Emmanuel Levinas, educational philosopher[30]

The Village Way educational community's **sky** is based on central, agreed-upon values encompassing a sense of meaning, purpose and holiness. We work with students as they cope with daily dilemmas, helping instill belief in their ability to make moral decisions and formulate a personal credo.

We use the term HELP to represent this concept because it suggests the way our teens' acting out is really a cry for help. Our role as educators is to help kids work through these issues by focusing on four values:

- Holiness: Values-based discourse for the person seeking meaning
- Ethics: Moral discourse: "That which is hateful unto you, do not do to your neighbor."
- Law: Basic discourse for the person who fears punishment
- Partnership: Educators and youth are partners in the process, not adversaries

Three Elements of Sky:

- Expressing **fundamental values** through flagship programs that unite the educational community
- Strengthening **identity** through values that are brought up during celebrations and discussion of holidays and festivals
- Advancing students in **levels of moral judgement** through ongoing discussion of ethical dilemmas

---

30 "Ethics and Infinity" [*Etica veHaensofi*] Translated into Hebrew by Efraim Meir (Jerusalem: Magnus Press, 1995)

CHAPTER 3

Circles of *Tikkun*: Repairing the Heart and the World

"The possibility for the home to open to the Other is as essential to the essence of the home as closed doors and windows."

—Emmanuel Levinas[31]

Individual *Tikkun* and Communal *Tikkun*

Many times, I have heard educators say: "We lack tools. We want to know how to deal with disciplinary problems!" Sometimes, we all crave some magic tools to make disciplinary issues disappear, so that we can focus on learning. We understand that they are an integral part of the educational process, but their frequency and intensity seem to require a response that does not exist or is not immediately available in our toolbox.

We know how to parrot sentences like: "Disciplinary issues are educational opportunities." We realize that they are the beating heart of the educational process—making way for growth—yet they always come up at the worst possible time. The truth is that there are no magic tools. We *are* the tools and can handle such problems effectively. Consistent expansion of our knowledge and awareness will help us to improve our ability to cope; so, with time, our response will improve and not lead to burnout.

The word *tikkun* is a Hebrew word with two central meanings: to improve and to repair. One form of *tikkun* is the process of continual

---

31 Emmanuel Levinas, *From Totality and Infinity: An Essay on Exteriority*, 1969

improvement in which a person is responsible for creating a better, more ethical reality. It focuses on the positive rather than pushing back on the negative; we identify a good core and seek to continue developing from that point. Another form of *tikkun* refers to something that has been broken and needs to be restored. These two different aspects are combined within the educational process, as well as in the process of human development.

Tikkun in the sense of improvement works like holistic medicine, strengthening the entire system and the healthy forces within it. *Tikkun* in the sense of repair is undertaken in a state of crisis. The two types strengthen one another. On the one hand, the more one focuses on that which is healthy, the less need there is to deal with repairing breakdowns. On the other, the more one learns from the difficulties, the more one strengthens the entire system.

This circular process incorporates **Tikkun HaLev** and **Tikkun Olam**, concepts from the Jewish mystical tradition. In the Village Way methodology, *Tikkun HaLev*, Hebrew for repairing the heart, refers to actions which present the teens with a sense of responsibility in their own lives, while *Tikkun Olam*, Hebrew for repairing the world, is the term for a sense of responsibility within the greater society, which we hope to help young people cultivate. The process calls upon teens to persistently act to progress as human beings while contributing to their immediate community and beyond. The **circles of** *tikkun* serve to deepen that which is good and rooted in our values, while also enabling learning and growth from our difficulties and moments of crisis. Each person takes responsibility for his own personal growth and for contribution to society.

Tikkun HaLev

Sharon, an educator at a Village Way school shares with us:

> *We used to call it "punishment." It used to be that when a child interfered in class, we treated his behavior as a nuisance. Today, the*

starting point is the tikkun process. We need to understand and analyze situations. What happened? Why is he in this place? How do we grow from here and continue forward? The whole approach has changed.

Sharon's words refer to *Tikkun HaLev* from crisis, which we as parents and educators are challenged by on almost a daily basis. Disciplinary problems lead to the moments when professionalism clashes with our instinctual response, when severe feelings of anger or disappointment overwhelm, and when it is difficult for us to see the *tikkun*, the healing, that is possible. Instead, we are focused on the crisis. When we practice looking through '*tikkun*-colored glasses' and act from within the circles of *tikkun*, we develop the ability to relate to disciplinary problems from a broader perspective, thus improving our responses. In this way, we establish a *tikkun* process, which at the beginning is intense and maybe even painful but eventually leads to growth and rewards. The disruptive child is expressing a yearning for meaning. Our challenge is to identify his call for help, his longing for meaning, rather than hearing it as just a battle cry. We need to remind ourselves of the essence of our mission as educators who have been taught to look to the future.

Sharon goes on to describe the process of *Tikkun HaLev*:

Throughout the educational process, we constantly refer to the student's strengths and only later raise the difficulties. This creates a change in the child. He is emotionally available to listen and to work hard to progress. This is also the case when dealing with parents. We start with conveying their children's strengths, which are a good basis for growth. We then move on to areas that need improvement. When working from a place of tikkun, from a place of meaning and empowerment, we see better results.

Her words illustrate the main stages of the *tikkun* process, which begin with the willingness of the educator, the student and the educational community to see the good, not only in the moral sense but in the practical sense, to identify the seeds of good, the 'anchors' that can be implemented in other areas of life.

How to Recognize the Positive

- **Identify Strengths and Good Deeds:** We create an educational community that seeks to see the specific, tangible good in each of its members, the areas in which they excel.
- **Recognize Strengths:** The discourse itself creates a space for strengths to be recognized and serves to enhance them through mirroring them back to the adolescent, among other methods. The adolescent needs to feel that adults see him in a positive light. This is something that he or she may not be used to and may find hard to believe, so persistence is crucial.
- **Create Experiences of Success:** It is crucial to create opportunities for students to express their strengths through performing, singing or dancing on stage; creating murals in public spaces; logistical responsibility for field trips; or leading the way in navigation exercises. We should abandon the idea that roles such as leading a hike or singing in the school show are rewards reserved for good students. They are educational opportunities and should be used widely.
- **Share Experiences of Success:** Sharing successes with the wider community is crucial. Public recognition by the educator and the educational community resonates with the student and helps him to identify himself as someone with strengths. In this process, the strengths become 'anchors' in the growth process.
- **Utilize Strengths Toward *Tikkun*:** The process of learning from successes takes place when we locate those who succeed, recognize and empower them, so they will function as catalysts for additional successes in other areas. So it goes in the *tikkun*

process, we utilize strengths to assist the young person and to improve in the specific areas we seek to change.

A Person Repairs the World and the World Repairs the Person

Building awareness of the strengths and weaknesses in our relationships teaches us to learn from every situation. In the process of *tikkun*, a person takes responsibility for his many virtues and shortcomings. He learns to accept himself and identify the values that are important to him and strives to further himself in a positive way. In *Tikkun Olam*, the individual and the community undergo a similar process by practicing how to accept the 'other' in a process of mutual responsibility. In this way, *a person makes his mark on the world, and the world is integrated within the person.*

It is not always easy for us to see the good. This may be due to a technical reason; for example, a teacher needs to engage a large group of students for a limited amount of time, and the focus is mainly imparting knowledge, not on internal growth, which limits the time available for identifying strengths. Aside from the technical, there are other barriers. We often encounter students in their role as those who either oppose or obey us, an impersonal dynamic that leaves us unable to see their strengths. Although their uniqueness may be hard to spot, we can recognize positive actions such as when they display consideration of others, sensitivity, initiative, and leadership. We can have a discussion with the members of the educational team and discover their strengths.

Interestingly, strengths can also be expressed through any number of unacceptable actions too—from drawing beautifully on a brand-new, wooden desk at school to effective leadership of friends in an act of mischief. Each educator has her own perspective of the child and can identify the good in different ways. Although, staff meetings are generally used to address failures (*tikkun* as repairing and not *tikkun* as improving), a truly supportive educational community seeks to move beyond this, to lead the discourse toward the success of every student.

As educators, we need to cherish the positive moments and draw strength from them. There are some students who by the first week of school are already involved in violence or rule breaking. But even then, the starting point should be that everyone has strengths and that we, as educators, have the duty to empower our students. Every child has the right to start their year with those surrounding him believing he will succeed. Everyone wants to succeed, but sometimes something fails along the way. This perceived failure can strengthen the bond between the educator and the student and create an eventual experience of success and *tikkun*.

> During the preparations for the new school year, I ask all staff members continuing with the same group of kids to make note of those who challenged them the previous year, specifying their strengths. As they write the lesson plans for the first two weeks, I ask that they include the goal: "To search for their successes." The starting point is that everyone begins the year with goodwill. Let students experience success and report it to their parents!

Tikkun connects to a search for meaning. It stems from the premise that every person acts out of this wish, even when their behavior is not to our liking. The *tikkun* process relates to a person's connection with his inner world, his motives, his points of expertise and the deepest parts of his identity. This applies to both successes and difficulties. Sometimes, behaviors perceived by us as negative, or against the rules, are defined by the teenager as successes. The educator needs to correct the behavior without diminishing the student, out of great respect for his potential. *This does not mean you give in to them.* There is a need for discipline, but from a place of meaning. For the most part, rebellion is part of the healthy growth process that takes place during adolescence. The challenge is to isolate the core of the child's strength and to channel it in a growth-oriented manner that will become meaningful to the young person too.

Finding Meaning in Discipline

A supportive adult often finds herself debating the appropriate pedagogical way to deal with boundaries that have been crossed, rule breaking and disciplinary problems. Every response, or lack of response, sends an educational message that our children internalize. Some say that any disciplinary violation has a hidden message from the child— a statement, a question or a call directed at the adults. The question of how we should respond to a young person who is testing boundaries is complex. The answer to the question is also complex; but to be clear—a response is crucial.

On the one hand, punishment is a strong statement both for the child being punished and for others in the community, as it expresses that we as adults trust him enough to hold him responsible. However, sometimes we realize that an instance of rule breaking expresses fear or distress, or is simply intended to get our attention. These issues bring into focus two modes of interaction between adult and youngster: discipline (*mishma'at*) and meaning (*mashma'ut*), two words that sound similar in Hebrew. Even on the issue of setting limits and how to respond, we should go on a 'case by case' basis. The same action by two different young people is likely to lead to two different, even opposite responses and, ultimately, to a completely different process.

Take the example of two Village Way communities in which students had thrown stones and caused damage to a building. Each community focused on a different value in dealing with the disciplinary problem.

The Rolling Stones

In one of the communities, a large stone was thrown into the classroom window and almost hit the teacher. At first, educators did not know who threw it. After a lengthy investigation, the thrower was identified, punished and suspended from school for several days. When he returned, he began a profound process of tikkun. The school principal explained to the whole community that there are boundaries of violence and disrespect that cannot be crossed. This demand, he explained, is rooted in respect for the students and their security and shows students what is important and what the community believes they can do.

In another school, on the morning of English language final exams, after many days of study and preparation, a boy threw a stone through a window in the dining hall and broke it. The principal explains:

It happened as we were going into breakfast. The window shattered into pieces, abruptly interrupting the morning calm. He stood there outside the dining room, bowed his head and said nothing. He did not try to escape and did not place the blame on anyone else. He tried to explain, but the feeling was stronger than words could express. There was something in his expression that explained everything, much more than any word that was said. The staff came right away to calm him down and support him, but most of all, to hug him. A half an hour later, he was sitting in the classroom, primed and ready. The test began. Ten months earlier, he had not even been ready to listen to anything about his studies or about his future. But not long before the final exam, he had received the highest grade in his class on the English practice test. The experience of success—even more than the grade—had made a lasting impact on him.

*

So, when he crashed the window, the immediate response of the community was to reach out to him and hug him. The staff realized that his was an emotional act, apparently stemming from the lack of ability to express all the emotions that were built up inside. They knew it was important to be there for him. The staff saw through his behavior to the fear and apprehension about the test, and they empathized with his loneliness and inability to verbalize the built-up emotions. They were familiar with the past he brought with him and the present he was dealing with. So, their response strengthened their relationship with him. At that moment of embrace, a tikkun was made for him that he had never received in any educational or family setting. And that boy, after he had burst into tears and calmed down, was then free to take the exam and pass it successfully. After a while, when things were quieter, he had to find a way to pay for the damage he caused, working together with maintenance personnel to build something positive for the community. Tikkun is not done just by bringing the situation back to its original state; it should leave things in a better place. It enables the adolescent to build an 'anchor,' a meaningful experience that will accompany him later in life.

Each of these stories presents a different response to a similar disciplinary problem. One is temporary exclusion from the community and the other is total containment, listening to motivations, needs and wants with an attitude of care. There is no right or wrong response so long as our actions do not stem from motives related to ego or, G-d forbid, revenge. In the first broken window case, the response was chosen to serve the overall educational climate as well as to respond to the boy's personal motivations. In the second case, it related more to the individual, observing the boy in the broader context of his life and his educational process. In both, the staff realized that the disciplinary issue was the child's way of saying "Look at me!" just as any severe disciplinary problem is a cry for help. We need to listen to what a young person's behavior is telling us and teach him that he can attract our attention in positive ways, not only through problematic behavior.

At times, our routine as an educational community is thrown off balance, which with proper guidance and direction, is essential for growth.

Punishment is also part of the process, part of *tikkun*. This does not mean being forced to pay a fine and then going about your day normally. Any penalty needs to be followed by a deep process of investigating the motives, clarifying the alternatives, and exploring the options for growth. Sometimes, we only treat the symptom and are not emotionally available to deal with the root of the problem, so that within a short time, the symptom is repeated. This happened in one of the Village Way schools:

> *At the end of one school day, when all the kids were ready to get on the buses, one of the boys threw a stone at a teacher. It was an intentional straight shot, but the teacher managed to duck out of the way. It was clear that the boy had crossed every boundary of proper behavior, and from the point of view of the educational community and its leadership, he would have to be expelled. Two weeks later, another stone was thrown at one of the teachers. This time, they did not know the identity of the culprit. The school principal called to consult with me, and at first, she was surprised to hear me say that I was glad she did not know who threw the stone. Why? Because now we would be obliged to carry out a comprehensive process throughout the entire school, if only to identify who threw the stone.*
>
> *The first stone-throwing by the buses crossed a red line. Clearly something terrible in the atmosphere there made it possible; and so, a community-wide tikkun process was needed that would involve those who saw the original stone-thrower approaching and did not stop him, as well as the wider group of all the students who heard about it. The day-to-day life of the community should have been put on hold to talk about the consequences of that first event. After the second stone was thrown, I felt it was crucial to undergo a communal process, even in the absence of the youth who threw the stone. All classes held discussions regarding the sanctity of human life, violence, its moral implications and the punishment expected by law for those who choose to be violent. The talks were accompanied by an educational program*

that included a parents' evening and a renewed signing of a code of honor, to which educators, parents and students were committed.

Disciplinary Problems as Opportunities

A disciplinary problem tells us much about the community. It is like a symptom that requires an in-depth treatment of *tikkun* and recovery. I always carry the story of Ayano with me as a cautionary tale.

Ayano was an outstanding student. At every staff meeting, we would mention his name, and the staff would agree unanimously that they had no problem with him, that everything was great and there was no need to spend time discussing him as we did for other "challenging" kids. We never encountered any disciplinary problems involving him and he earned every certificate of excellence possible. When Ayano graduated high school and went on to his compulsory duty in the Israeli army, he joined an elite army unit with three of his classmates. If they had allowed us educators to bet who among them would have finished the training course, we would all have bet on Ayano because the others had caused a lot of problems along the way. But during basic training, Ayano committed suicide. His story hit us hard. We were shocked. No warning bell had been heard. We felt that we had missed something big and were afraid that we had somehow collaborated with his disguise of good behavior. We failed because we did not realize that it was not normal for an adolescent who had experienced such difficult transitions in life to not act out or rebel. It is normal for an adolescent to test the limits, and we actually hope this will happen on our watch. Ayano's friends had challenged us and made it possible for us to travel with them through a process of growth. Ayano had also undergone a process that seemed significant to us, and we had also seen and guided him in different areas— and yet we missed something substantial. Only during the shiva mourning period were we exposed to the full scope of the difficulties

he had faced. Excellence and good behavior seemed to be his way to get
through high school, while pain was present underneath the facade.

One of the lessons learned from this painful case was that rather than be angry when young people break rules, we should thank those who have the strength to ring the warning bells, those who trust us to be there when they act out.

Ayano was not 'invisible' in the usual sense. We supposedly saw him, but not really. He was appreciated but he was not understood in a way that would enable him to unload some of the burdens he was carrying on his shoulders. This is not to say, G-d forbid, that every 'good' boy or girl is in distress. There are many ways to grow and progress, not all of them out of crisis, but we should do everything in our power to understand all our youth.

Who Sees the Invisible Kids?

There are 'invisible' boys and girls in our schools. We may think they are treated like everyone else, but the real test is how they perceive their place in their class or community. As part of the Village Way educator training sessions, we usually conduct an exercise with staff, asking them to write down the names of the students with whom they have a good relationship. A good relationship with a student is defined as knowing him personally, including what he is good at. We collect the names, and unfortunately, the number of children named is generally quite limited, and many names repeat themselves. These are the kids with whom it is easy to build a relationship; and sometimes, it is not their personalities but their difficult life stories that draws the staff to them. The next stage of the exercise is to take the list of children that no staff member has mentioned and divide them among members of the Village. Every adult is asked to add three or four teens to his list, to strengthen the relationship with them, to take an interest in them and to convey a message: *You are not invisible.* It is not only youth that feel invisible; even staff members may feel that way. The same exercise is therefore appropriate for school administration to express care for the staff.

In a different training session, we asked the school principal to include the security guard and the janitorial staff. We passed out candy in different colors to the whole staff and told everyone the rules of a game. Each staff member had to share an experience from their past to receive a candy. If someone shared about the smells or sounds from childhood, he or she would be rewarded with an orange candy. A red candy was for one's earliest memory. A janitor at the school of Ethiopian descent shared an emotional experience of personal empowerment, which made the teachers wish they had taken the time to get to know about this woman's powerful personal history earlier. During the following year, the teachers asked her to come into homeroom classes and share her story with the students. Her role grew with time. Four years later, I returned for a meeting at that school. The same woman greeted us and showed us her usual area where she sat with students and prepared hot tea for them, engaging with them and explaining to them that it was important to commit to their studies. She did this while also carrying out her responsibility for the cleanliness and warm, family atmosphere at the school.

Getting Thrown off Balance

Getting thrown off balance is — to a certain extent—the bread and butter of education. In other words, an essential part of the *tikkun* process takes place when the educational routine is interrupted by events, such as trips and special events, or on the other hand, by disturbances. The *tikkun* and growth take place as part of a balancing process. When one understands the meaning of the violation, one goes deeper and works toward progress.

Should I, as an educator, deliberately throw things off balance, or should I assume that the imbalance will occur on its own? There is no need to create crises, but there is certainly room to challenge the students to respond to complex situations on field trips and in lessons. This will make it possible to bring up existing difficulties and to talk to the students about the ethical and academic standards by which they must abide. I challenge them to deal with things in a way that creates a positive imbalance, bringing up difficulties for the purpose of growth.

Seeds of Tikkun

After the Mount Carmel forest fire in 2010, in which a large portion of Yemin Orde Youth Village was burned to the ground, people tried to comfort the staff by saying that it was an opportunity for growth. In retrospect, that was true; but at the time, it felt like a superficial saying that prevented us from being present in the crisis, allowing ourselves to fully feel the pain. To borrow an agricultural image, this kind of comment does not allow time to complete the process of decomposition in which the seed sheds its shell, so it can grow. Only by experiencing the crisis, accepting and internalizing it can we enable transformation of the painful components into hopeful thoughts and material for growth. This is also the case during times of crisis within an educational community. First, we need to be present in the crisis and not whitewash it. We must experience the difficulty and the pain, and only then, can we move forward. In general, our weaknesses as human beings, the difficulties we experience and the mistakes we make carry within them our greatest strengths. The young people in our lives test their limits and our own, as well as the rules of the adult world. A supportive adult is one who will react in a growth-oriented manner to that process. In other words, a community of meaning that guides youth through adolescence is engaged in a constant process of *tikkun*, one that involves the young people testing boundaries and searching for meaning, as the framework helps them consider how to behave in the world and the values that drive their actions.

Dr. Peri used to tell the kids at Yemin Orde that we see them as "noble." He explained that each letter of the word אציל *atzil* (the Hebrew word for noble) suggests qualities that are present in each of the young people: faith (אמונה *emunah*), justice (צדק *tzedek*), knowledge (ידע *yeda*), and a heart (בל *lev*) sensitive to others. Every year, we hold a 'Challenge Hike' for the seniors—a physically and emotionally difficult hiking trip, at the end of which we hold a ceremony where the seniors gives a class name to the freshmen. Over the years, the trip has brought up many opportunities to put our educational principles to work. Many disciplinary and behavioral issues came up. The worst case that I can remember was when a few kids drank alcohol during the hike. They replaced the water in their water jugs with vodka and reached the final ceremony dehydrated and inebriated. Visibly drunk, one of the kids began to yell out his own difficult story, that his mother died leaving him motherless. His informal educator approached him to hold him and calm him down, and in response, the youngster head-butted him. At the same time, a different student came up to me while I was leading the ceremony and grabbed the microphone out of my hand, and also drunk, said: "We look drunk to you, but we are really 'noble,' endowed with faith, justice, knowledge and a sensitive heart to others." That moment was both discomforting and meaningful. Even amid a grave mistake, the message was ingrained within them. They sought to remind everyone, and maybe even themselves, that they had good sides, that there were strengths that could be used to grow. Moments of rebellion and acting out are a key part of growing up. This story led to a meaningful process of *tikkun*, after which the kids went on another hike, this time behaving responsibly.

If You Broke It, You Can Repair It

Language creates reality, so instead of using punishment, we apply a process of *tikkun*. The difference is not merely semantic. The concepts differ in intent and procedure as well. Punishment takes immediate effect and temporarily restores social order. It is usually intended to hurt the person that did something forbidden. It is also there as a reminder, so when one is tempted to repeat his behavior, he is supposed to remember the pain and avoid it. All of us, both educators and parents, apply punishment as a pedagogical method on appropriate occasions. However, the Village Way sees punishment as far from ideal in that it often keeps teenagers stuck at the lowest level of moral judgment.

The essence of punishment is that it is immediate and conveys a clear-cut message regarding the *rule* that was violated. *Tikkun*, on the other hand, is a process that impacts the long term and relates mostly to the *value* that was violated. While punishment causes a person to feel small (at least at first), *tikkun* gives him the feeling that he is significant, but has made an error that needs to be corrected. In many situations in life, we know what is right but are impatient, hurt and angry, and so we go back to behavior that is familiar from our own childhoods—applying punishment. That is understandable, but not ideal. The *tikkun* process gives us a new way to approach such situations.

The Village Way DNA Process: A Meaningful *Tikkun* Process

Every disciplinary process begins with a young person who chose to break the rules. How do you respond? What do you do in real time? We have developed **the Village Way DNA Process** for just this purpose.

Clarification: The preliminary stage is a controlled response by the educator who witnessed the event. The purpose is to stop and make clear that something wrong has happened. A line has been crossed and we will not ignore it. The central message is: "That is not the way to act. You are much more respectable than the way you chose to act." It is important to remember that this is the first stage of the process and not the last. Therefore, comments like "You are done here." and "Watch your back." are not appropriate. The proper wording is: "Something problematic/serious/terrible has happened here. We will need to commit together to a process of *tikkun*."

To prevent misidentifying the person who crossed the line, we start with a short one-on-one conversation in which we ensure we have the right person. We clarify that something happened that will not allow us to return to business as usual without addressing the act with due seriousness, and we therefore take a time-out. This allows all sides to process what happened. This break can take two-to-three hours, or half-an-hour, or it can include suspension for one to three days, depending on the severity of the case. In most schools, suspension is punishment. For us, it is a time-out intended to be used as the beginning of the *tikkun* process. Before leaving for the break, the young person is asked to think about what happened, how to repair it, and what needs to happen for things to look better in the future. This process also grants time to consult with colleagues, offering a wider perspective that recalls the goals of the process as it also allows for creative thinking. It is likely that as educators, we will feel hurt on a personal level, a legitimate response. After all, we come to the task with all our hearts.

After the break stage, we set about the following steps in **The DNA Process: Dialogue, Negotiation, and Agreement.**

Dialogue: The dialogue begins with the message: *"We won't give up on you, so we don't give in to you,"* meaning—you crossed a line, but that is not what won't stop us from appreciating you and believing in you. Sometimes, the young person's action is difficult to accept due to its severity and this can be shared with him. The main goal of the dialogue is to clarify to the young person that we are on the same side, and that his success is our common goal. At this stage, we listen attentively to the youngster's version of events, trying not to conclude anything. It is important to try to understand his point of view. After we have heard his criticism of the staff, we say we'd be glad to discuss it another time but that the current meeting was scheduled due to his improper conduct. The dialogue stage can get bogged down in recounting the technical details of the event, but it is important to remember that repeating every detail is not necessary. We focus instead on what the child agrees was wrong and we try to understand him. What went wrong? What caused it? Maybe later, when the trust returns, the confession will expand. We need to clarify whether he understands that he committed a forbidden action; that is, does he know which rule he violated and why his action is forbidden? Which value is the rule intended to protect? Once we recognize the value and agree on its validity, we can move on to the next step.

Negotiation: This is the stage that opens discourse around the proposed response to the action. How does the young person suggest he repair what has been damaged? We must come up with creative and appropriate suggestions and be open to working out a plan with staff. Examine how the teenager responds to the *tikkun* offered him. Does he understand the connection between the response and the action? The proportionality is particularly important—large-scale public damage requires a large, public *tikkun*. Since the community has developed a negative impression of him due to the act, this will allow everyone to see him in a better light.

An educator might say: "You got drunk and acted violently in front of the whole school. You created a negative impression of yourself. I, as an educator, know that you are a person with values, leadership skills and the ability to speak to an audience, and I would like you to be recognized for the person you really are. What do you think would help to give others a more fitting impression of you?" You might suggest that the student lead a workshop about alcohol and its risks during homeroom. Perhaps he or she could gather students and organize volunteer work in cooperation with organizations that help those harmed by alcohol. In any case, the process should be timebound, with a clear task list.

Agreement: This step is an empowering end to the conversation. All involved meet on the day agreed upon in the previous stage and look at the entire process they have gone through together. Now, we can give positive reinforcement, look at the strengths of the young person that we uncovered during the *tikkun* and understand that we came out of the process much stronger than when we began. We set expectations for the future, clarify that we believe in the young person's abilities, and reflect the success back to him and to his family.

The complex 'DNA process' may be disruptive to the routine, especially in an environment in which a new disciplinary event develops every day. At the same time, experience shows that it has a positive effect on the educational climate, the lives of the teens and our sense of meaning as parents and educators.

There is a well-known parable about a man who spends so much time chasing after his horses that he does not have time to build fences. We do not want to be like him, and therefore we make the effort to find the time for the process—at the very least for severe infractions. Even if we do not quite succeed in implementing the process for every event, we would like each young person to experience one such process from start to finish. If that does not happen, we maintain our commitment to including a dialogue component in any disciplinary process, so that we can understand the adolescent's point of view. Neither do we give up on the principle that there needs to be reparative actions to back up the talk. The action component of *tikkun* is crucial to the young person's self-perception. She must come out on top after her fall and not just return to the starting point. Once the young person is actively involved in conducting workshops, assisting staff members in their jobs and connecting with others, and after she receives positive feedback, she may feel better and grow accordingly.

From Loss to Gain: Summary

Disciplinary problems are disruptions that present opportunities for children and adolescents to progress. We seek to leverage the educational opportunity within an apparent loss. In dealing appropriately with disciplinary problems, we offer young people the sense of meaning they are eager to find.

How to Turn a Loss into a Gain: What do You Need?

- An educational community with clear values and a set of expectations and rules that everyone knows ("It takes a village to raise a child.")
- An educator who identifies the young person's strengths and shares them with him and the community ("Every child needs an adult to believe in him.")
- A reparative *tikkun*-based educational response consisting of dialogue, action and conclusions. This includes:
  - Listening to the teen's motivation for his actions
  - Discussing and clarifying the rule that has been violated and the consequences
  - Identifying the value that has been disrespected through a discussion of why the rule and similar ones exist
  - Requiring the teen to improve his own self-perception as well as the community's perception of him
  - The educator and the adolescent working together to draw conclusions from the process

What Does a Teen Need—Boundaries or Acceptance?

Of course, we know that adolescents need both. But which is more important? How do we decide which is the priority? We seek to create the appropriate balance, but in the end, we need to decide whether we accept the child at all costs or condition the acceptance upon the boundaries we have defined. In a family, it is clear to almost everyone that the acceptance is far stronger than the boundaries, although this too has a limit. But what is appropriate in an educational community? In one of my conversations with a youth village director, he said: "Maybe we actually do them a disservice by accepting them at all costs? Maybe they instead need a kind of wake-up call, because everywhere else they will have to get their act together and behave accordingly. Maybe this approach would be a better gift for life."

My response was: A. Maybe. B. Kids who have come to study in your youth village have already suffered many blows in life from their friends, teachers, and other adults. We need to create an experience they are not used to, one in which they anticipate acceptance, despite their actions, an experience in which they must deal with the problems they have caused, knowing that the adults in their lives will not give up on them. The chance that such a "wake-up call" will straighten the child out is low, and sometimes it may even function as the straw that breaks the camel's back, leading to complete despair and dysfunction. But let's go back to the question of what a teen needs more: boundaries or acceptance? In a home where acceptance is natural, absolute, and clear, our main effort should be to set limits. But in an educational community founded on laws, rules and regulations, the main effort should be on acceptance while still maintaining a constant balance of repercussions for wrong behavior.

The Pros and Cons of Prevention Programs

In many schools, there are programs designed to reduce negative behavior by students. The Israeli Ministry of Education offers a recommended sampling of prevention programs: drugs and alcohol prevention, violence prevention, and more recently, prevention of shaming and cyberbullying. These programs are designed for all schools because every school is exposed to these problems. If we examine them in depth, we will find that most of them are excellent programs that encourage emotional strength, decision-making, health and leadership. However, as mentioned, language is a significant component of the educational process, and the title chosen for the program may be harmful even if the activity is useful. A student who comes to an activity on drug and alcohol prevention knows that this is something to be wary of, but subconsciously, he may think: The educators have brought me to an alcohol prevention program because they see me as a potential alcoholic. They do not really see a positive future for me. They see my pathology, rather than my strengths.

If we give these programs positive names, using terms such as "resilience" and "leadership," or "life skills," they will serve the overall goal better and encourage teens to participate. Using the term "prevention" can cause students not to attend, and even produce vocal rejection to the idea of such a program. On the other hand, sometimes we need to call a spade a spade, such as in therapeutic or rehab groups, where the stated goal is coping with addiction. In such groups, the name should include the word "prevention," but we recommend adding more positive terminology as well.

A teenager's process of searching for identity also includes testing boundaries that do not relate to their inner experience. In fact, some children and adolescents still do not fully grasp the most basic rule of life, that actions have consequences. Through rebellion, they experience the rules of life, becoming aware of their own powers and examining the powers of the adults who guide them. Adolescents often have sharply attuned intuition that allows them to identify a weakness in the rules at home, at school and in the society in which they live, as well as the weaknesses of their parents, educators and other adults.

Although sometimes it seems like all teens want to do is undermine our authority, that is not actually their intention. They want to roar in front of us as loudly and ferociously as possible, and still see us standing strong against it. Our ability to respond wisely to their provocative behavior reinforces their confidence in us as role models and guides. For the most part, we don't understand this, at least not in the moments we are tested. We tend to view their rebellions as a personal affront to us. Sometimes, we interpret the rebellion as a rejection of the values that we wish to convey to the next generation, and thus see it as a personal failure. When experiencing it this way, rebellion by the young people in our lives harms our self-perception and self-confidence to an almost unbearable degree.

Tikkun Olam

Tikkun HaLev has a profound, reciprocal relationship with *Tikkun Olam*. The two feed into each other and foster growth in individuals and in society. In both, there is constant striving for a more ethical life on both an individual and communal level. In addition to the individual *Tikkun HaLev*, there is significant value in engaging in *Tikkun Olam*, which in its simplest sense is rooted in social engagement and giving. We believe that every needs to engage in *Tikkun Olam*, just as they need to learn mathematics, history, and English. We use this term instead of "volunteering." For us, social engagement and giving is not something one does by choice, but as a required part of the curriculum. Our goal is to ensure that the graduates of our educational process contribute to the community. We hope that in the future our graduates will choose to engage in community service *voluntarily*, but while they are students, we provide meaningful *mandatory* community service experiences.

The Difference Between a Mirror and a Window

The third Village Way educators' conference that we conducted was dedicated to the tension between *Tikkun HaLev* and *Tikkun Olam*. We thought about, debated and tried to decide on a priority between the two. We chose to consider the options by studying the story of the glasscutter together:

> One evening, a glasscutter sat at home, opened a window and looked at the town around him. In earlier years, he had cut the glass for the large windows in each of the houses; but recently, he had been asked to install shutters on these windows so that people could have more privacy. As darkness fell, he saw that his neighbors were closing their shutters; in the streets, the poor members of their community were looking for food and shelter, with no one to see them and come to their aide. He felt sorry for his role in this and sighed. He thought about how these days, he only received orders of mirrors rather than windows. He was also troubled by the fact that the local synagogue would be fitted with lights and air vents, and thus would no longer need windows.

During the session, we asked the educators: Is it right to require teens to give back to the community as part of the curriculum? Resources are limited, and when there are gaps in areas such as knowledge, learning and life skills, these need to be attended to. Is it not better to invest our time and money into filling these gaps? This begs a larger question: Why should the students be giving time to others when they are missing out on so many things? Perhaps it is better to build their own selves up, so that in the future they will be able to give more to society? Or, using the terminology of the Village Way, first they should complete *Tikkun HaLev* and then afterwards go on to *Tikkun Olam*.

In answering this question, we may recall that the Village Way's third basic principle is that young people seek meaning. Some find it in expanding their knowledge, others in dreams for the future; but the broadest common denominator that speaks to every teen is *Tikkun Olam*. We create such opportunities simply because they contribute to the empowerment of our students.

Since time and resources are limited, efforts should be made to create priorities. Sometimes an opportunity to give can take the place of a lesson in which the student already excels, physical education, or one of his extracurriculars. We should not offer extra study sessions during the timeslot reserved for social engagement and giving activities because we miss a significant opportunity to meaningfully influence the children's lives. Adolescence is a significant stage in the formation of identity, and it is important that there be tangible experiences of formative social giving at this stage of life. The personal process of *Tikkun HaLev* never ends, and when it does not develop together with *Tikkun Olam*, it will always be lacking.

The Ability to Give and Receive

The essence of *Tikkun Olam*, as well as *Tikkun HaLev*, is the empowerment of good in the world and growth on the social and public levels. The ability to give and to receive is important in human interactions. This greatly influences teens and creates connections imbued with meaning, caring, and a sense of belonging.

Many schools work to give back to the community. Disadvantaged families, lone soldiers and bereaved families are hosted at youth villages during vacations and holidays. Often, the families of the kids at the village who have no other place to celebrate come as well. As hosts, our young people have the opportunity to give and to practice being members of the community. As Smadar, an educator, points out: "It is important that the students can leave the bubble and understand they can fit in as citizens in the future. We want them to feel they belong, so we encourage contributing to the community. We want students who are accustomed to being on the receiving end to internalize a perspective of giving and community involvement."

At the Village Way gap-year leadership program for young women located on Kibbutz Merhavia, in Israel's northern region, participants took it upon themselves to document the immigration stories of the local elderly. In another community, students and volunteers went out on a particularly rainy day to distribute food to the homeless in Tel Aviv. In yet another community, 12th graders decided to help children with special needs throughout the year. In some technical schools, students studying hair styling and cosmetology provide hairdressing and makeup services to members of a retirement community. There are also communities that open vocational workshops in the school to the elderly and disadvantaged. These actions empower the students and deepen their sense of belonging, meaning and personal responsibility.

April 2006. Spring had sprung and blossomed. The preparations for Passover were in full swing. We were engrossed in the act of ridding the campus of leavened products. The Passover theme of freed slaves somehow drifted to current events as we read in the newspaper of a group of youth imprisoned in the south of Israel, boys who had fled from distant African countries and been caught in Egypt, where they were traded as slaves before finding their way into Israel. Some called them refugees, others migrant workers. For us, they were a group of 15-16-year-olds, who had witnessed the loss of their family, fled their homeland and were imprisoned because they wanted to survive. The thought of Tikkun HaLev and Tikkun Olam led us to add six of these young men to our educational community. The seder of 2006 was extra meaningful for us and for anyone who heard our story about a religious Jewish youth village that chose to be blessed with newly liberated Muslim boys. They were not exactly free because their official status in Israel had not yet been settled, but shortly after their arrival, the suspicion surrounding the young men began to be tempered by a sense of their belonging with us. I was privileged to be part of the process that started with many doubts, as well as technical and ethical questions. Through it all, I experienced educational and spiritual experiences that put me in mind of the works of philosopher Emmanuel Levinas, who defined divinity as an encounter with the proverbial 'other.'

A decade later, In the spring of 2017, we accompanied Gassim Barry, one of the boys who had joined our community before going on to university, to his final resting place. During his university studies, Gassim had fallen ill and died. Naturally, our connection with him had continued after he graduated, and had received an additional layer of support because many staff members felt a soul connection with him. At a Muslim cemetery in Jaffa, a funeral according to Islamic tradition was held. After Gassim's burial, prayers and eulogies were held in Arabic, English, Swahili, French and Hebrew. Dozens of educators, friends from the Youth Village, university, and his neighborhood in south Tel Aviv were in attendance, Jews, Muslims, and Christians, all sad and all hopeful. Before leaving, one of his friends said, "Look at the cemetery. There are weeds, thorns, and a lot of garbage. Let's meet the day after tomorrow at 8 AM and clean the place in honor of our brother Gassim and in honor of all who are buried here." In that moment, I learned another lesson in Tikkun Olam from a group of refugees, for whom the most natural thing to do would have been to worry about their own survival.

Tikkun Olam as a Way of Life

Tikkun Olam is not hierarchical but cyclical. Anyone can find themselves giving or receiving. This is significant for the entire community. The effect of giving on a person may come from a meaningful one-time experience, but usually the individual act has limited influence (although even one-time giving is important, and a limited framework of giving is preferable to a routine life devoid of it).

Take the Israeli custom of donating sweets to hospital patients and the elderly before the holidays. We can ask ourselves whether the outcome of our act is indeed positive. Will the donut benefit the patient or the elderly person? It would appear the visit and the joy it engenders is the main gift, not the treat itself. But precisely for this reason, it is important that we continue this activity regularly and not just for holidays. In the past, a "personal commitment" activity was compulsory in Israeli schools only in the 10th grade. Here, too, a somewhat confusing message was conveyed—that the activity of giving is of value for one year only and all other ages are exempt. Happily, the Education Ministry expanded their activities through 12th grade and instituted a social service matriculation certificate for students who give back to the community more than 120 hours over 3 years.

In my time as an educator, there were years when we were satisfied with only sporadic experiences of *Tikkun Olam* due to budget and staff constraints. We recognized that we were missing out on something. Then, there was one year in which we were able to integrate all giving activities, so that without adding to our budget or manpower, we were able to create a powerful *Tikkun Olam* community:

> *That year the 12th grade chose to direct their Tikkun Olam activities to Israeli Prisoners of War (POWs) and MIAs (Missing in Action). Soldiers Gilad Shalit, Ehud Goldwasser and Eldad Regev were in captivity, and the entire country had mobilized for their release and in support of their families. We challenged the class by asking: Many people are working on this issue. What unique form of help can you*

*offer? The kids thought about it and answered that they did not want to do something **for** the families, but **with** the families. They were given the task of procuring contact information for the families and making initial contact with them. The first family member to answer was Miki Goldwasser, Ehud's mother. The students invited the families to hike with them at the end of their annual Challenge Hike and to be present at the year's closing ceremony. These moments were emotional for the entire community since the group regularly prayed for the welfare of their sons. It became the community project for the 12th grade. We invited the families into the project as we wrote a special prayer for Hanukkah that mentioned the prisoners and the missing soldiers. Concern for the safety of these young men permeated every aspect of our social and educational reality. On all the official Yemin Orde correspondence during that time—logo, invitations, greeting—there was a mention of the POWs and MIAs.*

When the deaths of Eldad and Ehud became known, Shlomo Goldwasser, Ehud's father, arrived at his son's funeral wearing the hat that had been designed and given to him before the hike with Yemin Orde. We did not give it much thought at the time. We assumed it had been by chance that he put it on. But when a group of educators and former students came to console the mourners at the shiva, Shlomo Goldwasser noticed us, and even though he was in the middle of a conversation with Knesset members and other dignitaries, he came over and hugged everyone. He was glad to see the graduates. He was very emotional and told us that it was no coincidence that he wore our hat during the funeral. "The strength you gave us on that hike was so meaningful, thank you, thank you," he kept saying. On the way back from the shiva, one of the older graduates said to his friend, "Do you get it? We gave him strength! We, of all people, gave him strength!"

As educators, we must recognize our almost unique opportunity to help our students progress from the position of receiving to the position of giving, thereby developing a self-perception that expresses: "We are not at the bottom of society's food chain. We belong to those who are making a difference and contributing to society."

Belonging to a *Tikkun Olam* Community

In choosing the right type of giving activity, we should adapt to the needs and wants of the students and educators. For example, there may be a certain reluctance to working with those with severe disabilities due to the emotional energy that requires. Likewise, educators who in their private lives are dealing with elderly parents needing round-the-clock care may find it difficult to care for the elderly. Some youth prefer food distribution activities as those do not require a human encounter, but for others, such projects may cause a sense of shame and be a reminder of times when their family lacked food. It is important to be aware of these kinds of issues when selecting the type of activity. Nonetheless, many educators ultimately choose the more intense interactions after realizing the great impact such experiences have on the students. For our part, we strive to allow every child to have human encounters because we know that by getting in touch with our discomfort, we can only grow. Many kids have discovered their sensitive and considerate sides because of encountering individuals with severe disabilities. Take the following story of a student who objected to a certain *Tikkun Olam* activity, but later revealed that he was particularly moved by it.

> We at Yemin Orde sometimes host children and adults with disabilities at our village, and invite them to use our pool. One of the students told us he was offended by the people who swam in the pool, and sometimes drooled while doing so. He felt that the village was a home for students and that the people with disabilities should not be hosted there. At the time, our reaction was multilayered. On the one hand, we were pleased that the boy felt a connection to the community and had the confidence to express his feelings. On the other hand, we were

committed to educating the students to contribute to others and to feel
that they have something to give. The boy was given the opportunity
to express his protest; however, we made it clear that although we
respected him, we expected him to deal with the fact that we would
continue to host these individuals. Years later, that boy, now an adult,
came with his children to show them where he had been educated.
He met the Village director and said excitedly to his children: "You
know what we did here? We did not just go on our cellphones and
computers like you … We hosted people with disabilities in the pool
and in the dining room …" In the end, what he had most opposed
became a significant part of his identity, his sense of belonging and
the collective memory he was carrying. This was the very thing he
wanted to convey to his children, his sense of belonging to a Tikkun
Olam community.

An educational team often asks itself how to make the acts of giving meaningful and how to respond to objections from the students. Experience shows that students are mostly excited to engage in *Tikkun Olam*. And once they have experienced it, they are more willing to be involved with it than other informal activities. Teens that are actively engaged often take ownership and find they are deeply connected to these activities. In many cases, discipline leads to meaning, so we have the responsibility to create the proper structure for the act of *tikkun* and help the students to maintain it.

To that end, we make use of the organizational structures to create the framework for this ongoing activity. The very act of enabling students to choose how they want to contribute leads to a profound sense of meaning. The *tikkun* circles are deeply embedded in the organizational structures of the educational community and influence its essence. When *Tikkun Olam* appears in the annual calendar at the class-, grade-, and school-wide levels, it affects the conversations among students and the way in which the educational community is perceived in the neighborhood and larger community.

Tikkun Olam Day

Our day-to-day life is busy. We need to make special time for things that are important to us. Although a relationship with parents is often part of our routine, we also create special events such as parent meetings or family day to ensure we make time for them. In the same spirit, it is appropriate to dedicate a special day for a community-wide *Tikkun Olam* event, a day when all members of the village stop their normal routine to participate in giving. Such a day is different than the ongoing *Tikkun Olam* activities, in which each group of students goes with its own educator at a set time to volunteer—and often does not choose how they will contribute. At the annual event, we try to create groups of giving-by-choice, with each group composed of members of the maintenance staff, educators, students and sometimes graduates.

Tikkun Olam Day or Good Deeds Day?

Good Deeds Day, a day of community service launched in 2007 to encourage good works in society, has taken its place on the Israeli calendar. Today every 'self-respecting' Israeli company or organization goes out with their workers to help a disadvantaged population on that day. Perhaps *Tikkun Olam* Day could be combined with Good Deeds Day—but this would require us to ask some questions.

The very name Good Deeds Day indicates that on all other days we are exempt from doing them. Of course, this is not the intention, but in the absence of proper explanations, language produces reality. Therefore, we should treat this day as the culminating event of ongoing activity, not as a one-off.

The good deed that is done on that day generally meets the need of a person or organization that is lacking. The recipient is happy with the joy of a need filled, and the giver feels the deep, meaningful joy of giving. It is precisely for this reason that the giver may want to replicate this feeling and therefore develop an ongoing plan to do good deeds that, ultimately, may benefit the givers more than the recipient.

How Do We Switch Roles?

How should educators react when companies want to hold their Good Deeds Day activities benefiting youth-at-risk? Renovating a clubhouse, classroom, or basketball court is something we can agree would be helpful, but it is important that we not remain in the position of the receiving party. We can leverage our approach by using the following principles:

- *Doing Good Together*: Ideally, we should use the budget and work force of the volunteers, together with our students, to help a third party, out of a joint sense of generosity that will lead to ongoing reciprocity. An educational community's administrators and educators will probably find it difficult to pass up the offer of a renovation of student lounges, classrooms, or sports facilities, if that is offered. If that does happen, and we agree to the offer, it is important to talk to the students about a respectable way of receiving that does not perpetuate their role as the needy party. It is an opportunity to share with them that every person has the need to both give and receive. To this end, we should ensure that the teens be involved in some way in the renovation, construction and painting of the parts of the school to which the funding is going.
- *Reciprocity:* The students—acting on the school's behalf—can reciprocate by paying a visit to volunteers who helped them. They can go to the offices of the company at which the volunteers are employed and offer to lend a hand. They can bake cakes or prepare soft drinks to refresh the workers in the middle of a day's work, during any regular day— and not because it is Good Deeds Day. We, as educators, need to understand that we are responsible for the proper use of such a day. Do good deeds reduce social gaps or perpetuate them? How we receive and give in return will decide that.

In one of the Village Way educational communities, a request came in from a unit of IDF soldiers to hold their Good Deeds Day event at the community's campus. The principal thought that it was not appropriate for the soldiers to volunteer at the school because it might reinforce the students' feeling of neediness. The students had been volunteering regularly at a center for the elderly and mentally ill, and so instead, the principal and the unit's commander decided to organize a joint trip, in which both the soldiers and the students would travel to the Western Wall in Jerusalem with the elderly. Some of the elderly were Holocaust survivors so traumatized by their histories that they were living in a closed psychiatric ward, rarely granted an opportunity to leave the institution.

Due to a technical mistake, the students missed the bus they had been meant to take, so the elderly people arrived on their own bus. The students waited for them at the Western Wall Plaza together with the soldiers. When the bus carrying the elderly came into the Plaza, the students and soldiers brought wheelchairs over to help the excited and somewhat shocked patients. Fear and discomfort were evident on the faces of the students and soldiers, but the fact that the two groups of young people were working together put them all at ease. The school director noted that a Torah reading was taking place in one of the prayer quorums at the Western Wall, and it lacked a cohen, a member of the priestly class needed for the reading. The gabbai, the individual managing the prayers, called out: "Is there a cohen here?"

Suddenly, one of the Holocaust survivors, who had been hospitalized for years in a closed ward, detached from his environment and non-verbal, raised his hand quite naturally and said, "I am a cohen." The therapists looked at him in astonishment and asked: "Are you a cohen?" He requested that one of the teens lead him to where they were reading the Torah. He kissed the Torah scroll and began saying the Torah blessing by heart, after which he raised his hands above the students and soldiers and gave them the priestly blessing: "May the LORD bless you and protect you! May the LORD deal kindly and graciously with you! May the LORD bestow His favor upon you and grant you peace!"

For the young people, this was a very meaningful experience, even before the educators helped them to process it. They felt this even more when an educator reflected on what a big privilege and opportunity this had been. This man had remembered his past, that he was a cohen. A man who was a child during the Holocaust had apparently had his first aliyah to the Torah in the Jewish State while visiting the Western Wall, thanks to their involvement.

Within such moments of giving, there are experiences of success that deepen the sense of community and the individual's *Tikkun HaLev*. What is particularly important in this story is that the worshippers were missing a cohen, and the community needed one and his blessing. The students and staff had the opportunity to experience the highest level of giving. Beyond just giving to someone, they were able to witness the recipient also giving back.

Dilemmas Surrounding *Tikkun Olam*

Moving away from the self and toward the 'other' is a necessary step in the search for meaning, as discussed in an earlier chapter about the 'sky' element. Growth in moral discernment comes from confronting ethical dilemmas. The more we engage in thought and discussion, the more we will improve our judgment when making ethical decisions. Therefore, even in dealing with *Tikkun Olam*, we need to ask questions.

Educated Giving

Sometimes someone wants to help, but the potential receiver conveys disinterest in receiving. How do we know when it is right to give and when to hold back? How can we make sure that this consideration—that the other person does not really want our help—does not serve as an excuse allowing us to take the easy way out?

We need to think of moments when we ourselves were in need, to connect to that experience of need, and out of sensitivity, help others. We must try to ensure that our giving comes from the right place, that we know people are only weak at certain times in life. There is no one who is always weak, and no one who is never weak. We might encourage students to say: "In the past, I received, and now, it is my prerogative to give. Now it is your turn to receive. Pay it forward when you can."

Shuli, an educator in a technological school, participated in the Village Way professional educators' forum for those working on community service and Tikkun Olam projects in their schools and villages. As at every Village Way meeting, we began with a text learning session. We tried to understand why. We talked about respectful giving and how to give and still succeed in preserving the respect of the recipient. We said that the ability to receive is a sign of strength.

Shuli's eyes shone when she heard this sentence. I could see she was debating whether to say something. When we asked staff members to share a personal experience of when they were in need, Shuli asked to speak and related that six years earlier, she and her family found themselves in an extremely difficult economic situation. She worked as a teacher, but the income was not enough for basic needs. After much deliberation, she gathered her strength and appealed to a charity organization for help with food. Her eyes watered as she shared her difficulty in providing her daughters with basic needs, wondering how to explain to them the origin of the care package that appeared. She told us that she and her girls would take the packages of food they received, prepare a smaller package, and pass it on to someone else who was also in need.

Six years later, Shuli and her family's situation had greatly improved, and as far as she was concerned, it was only natural that she now concentrate on school projects involving giving to others. Shuli's ability to share this story with her colleagues attested to her personal resilience, which brought up the thought that in some way, all of us, both students and educators, are disadvantaged at times. Finally, Shuli said: "What helped us maintain our dignity was the discretion with which people helped us, and the fact that even in our difficult situation, we gave to others from the little we received. That is why it is so important that we let our students give, and that we do it with respect for all. "

The Act of Giving Shapes the Giver

Should one person be given a large sum of money that can significantly change his life, or should many people be given a small sum? On a personal level, I tend to say that it is better to help one person significantly than to make a symbolic contribution to many people. But as an educator, I think, following the writings of Maimonides, that it is better to let students experience a thousand smaller acts of giving rather than one large, reality-changing act. This thinking is based on the realization that a person's emergence from the cycle of poverty does not really depend on one source of help. We do not have the ability to change someone's reality from one extreme to the other, but we do have control over our actions, and the very act of giving shapes the identity of the giver. This is *Tikkun Olam* that serves *Tikkun HaLev*. The act of giving turns us into better people.

The Poor of Your City

Every time a difficult event occurs in the world, a natural disaster or a war, a question arises in the educational context: What can we do for people in distress? Usually a counterargument is immediately raised, quoting the Jewish scriptural injunction that the poor of your city take precedence over those from other cities.[32] Those who hold that view have verbalized it during such recent global tragedies as the 2010 earthquake in Haiti, the recent earthquake in Turkey, and lately, the bloody battles in Syria.

---

32 Tractate Bava Metziah: 71a

The question can be applied to the entire concept of *Tikkun Olam*. Why is it necessary at all? Let us stick with *tikkun* of the person. One could say that before we go renovate the homes of the elderly, we should renovate stairwells in the students' homes at the village.

Here we must ask, which of our actions will serve our educational purpose? If the kids themselves become the object of such help, they may label themselves as "poor" or, G-d forbid, a "parasite." In this context, the students may think of "poor" as someone who shamefully accepts help and does not believe that he can get out of his situation. A "parasite" for them may be someone who accepts shamelessly, and perhaps even demands, yet has no interest in escaping his situation. But we are preparing our students to break the glass ceiling that always appears to be falling on them. "Parasites" and "ashamed, poor kids" cannot break through the glass ceiling. Only those who can connect with others, look far into the future, and act for the greater good will be able to break through.

It is true that there is a great difference between aid within our society and assistance to a foreign people. An act of giving within our immediate community may not really allow us to see the 'other,' but merely a reflection of ourselves. The more we give to those at a distance, the more our students will be able to see the distant 'other' in his distress and do something about it. This process also grants them the ability to return to their own neighborhoods, noticing problems they had not seen before and trying to solve those as well.

Unfortunately, natural disasters will always be a part of life. The terrible disaster that struck Haiti and exacted a high human toll could have remained in the background of our educational activity since it was not part of our informal education program, and certainly not part of the curriculum. We could have dedicated a lesson to it and then returned to routine. But out of a commitment to finding meaning in all events, we chose to hold a community gathering to raise awareness and pray for the safety of the missing, especially the children. During the gathering, the Village leader asked the student council to formulate ideas on how students could help Haitian children who were injured. The council met and decided to collect five shekels from every student, but they were surprised that their appeal to the Village administration to approve the plan was not approved. The administration's reason: "Five shekels is theoretically not very much money, but not every act of giving should come down to giving money. We would like to be involved in other causes, and it would not be fair to collect money from everyone multiple times as everyone has a different economic situation."

Faced with this roadblock, the council met again with representatives from the staff, and then the idea came up to ask Avi, the kitchen and dining hall manager, how much money was spent each month on buying croissants. Avi showed them an invoice for 6,400 shekels. The student council decided to give up croissants for a month and send the money to the victims of the disaster. The Village administration welcomed the initiative, but asked that all the students sign a document stating explicitly that they were giving up croissants for the benefit of the children who were injured in the disaster in Haiti. The council felt that was unnecessary, and that it had the authority to make such a decision, but the administrators felt that signing such a document would create a feeling of partnership among the kids. After the youth of the Village signed the document, we sent a check for 6,400 shekels to victims of the Haiti disaster.

Tikkun Olam as an Educational Process

The experience of the youth as partners in *Tikkun Olam* depends on the act of giving, but it also depends on how the educators process the experience with them. Preparation for the experience and further activities at its conclusion require effort, yet this extra work will help us achieve the maximum benefit.

Before embarking on an activity, we need to broaden our students' knowledge and connection to the chosen topic. We should describe the destination, projected tasks and how the strengths of everyone will be expressed. It will also help students if we allow them to raise their concerns about the activity, including the difficulties that may arise. We might spend some time role-playing regarding what to expect. Usually *Tikkun Olam* activities require guidance through every step—for example, in this experience at a nursing home:

A group of girls, some of Ethiopian descent, went to volunteer in a nursing home. In preparation, we dealt with questions that were bothering them. At first, we spoke about their reluctance to work with the elderly, and about what it may have meant for these senior citizens to have moved to a nursing home. Afterwards, we spoke about the possibility of sexist, disrespectful comments, and how to respond, and we held simulations such as: What will you do if you go up to someone and he calls you a derogatory term or says: "Don't touch me?" We spoke of possible feelings that may arise and a choice of responses. Given that these were elderly people who might lack inhibitions, we asked: Who is stronger in this situation? How should we respond or feel? These issues were of real concern to the young women, who were about to enter an unfamiliar situation. During the volunteering, an elderly man did indeed shout: "What's this? They brought us Negroes?" One of the young women responded with sensitivity and great dignity: "I understand you. You are not used to this. I wish you well."

Just as preparation for an encounter is necessary, it is just as important to process the event afterwards through an open discussion of feelings and sharing meaningful experiences, including which points of strength were discovered. Afterwards, we can share these experiences with the wider community. We can talk about the activities during ceremonies, in letters to the parents and on bulletin boards with pictures alongside quotes from students. In this way, even those who did not participate can feel a part of a community that does good deeds.

As noted, *Tikkun Olam* deepens the experiences of meaning by fostering a feeling of responsibility, belonging, and involvement of the person in society. Belonging to a *Tikkun Olam* community creates a feeling of meaning which remains throughout the years.

To 'Plant' the World in the Person

Another meaningful part of the ongoing educational process of *Tikkun Olam* is the actual encounter with the 'other' and the opportunity to widen our students' perspectives. Using a metaphor from the world of agriculture, we at the Village Way call this "to plant the world" in the person by expanding horizons, instilling curiosity and knowledge in a way that moves across cultures.

Adolescents alternate between having healthy natural curiosity and being apathetic. It can be said that as digital memory has expanded in our smartphones, the memory in our brains has been reduced. Since all necessary knowledge can seemingly be accessed with a click, we remain ignorant. But even in this reality, we know that knowledge is power and that it plays a significant role in a teen's self-perception. We must therefore stimulate curiosity in every possible way and try to broaden horizons in creative ways. *Tikkun Olam* projects are opportunities to enrich the world of our teens. They enable us to 'plant,' to instill, the world within them. We are not random molecules in space. We are part of a larger world, and the more we know about that world—including facts and information—the more we increase what the world can offer us.

Once, when preparing for a *Tikkun Olam* visit to a hospital, we held activities to familiarize the kids with the names of the departments and specializations. Each student received a question sheet: What is an oncology department? What does it treat? What is neurology? What is the difference between neurology and urology?

In a similar fashion, when we went out to pick fruit for needy families, we taught agricultural concepts. We examined root vegetables and learned about the difference between dryland and irrigation farming. It was a wonderful opportunity for kids from farming backgrounds to demonstrate their knowledge and to share the methods used in their countries of origin. We talked about the state's responsibility vis-à-vis the responsibility of nonprofit organizations, and whether assistance from the nonprofit sector is totally positive or allows the state to shirk their responsibility.

When we went to work with the aged, we learned about the elderly in Israeli society and asked what differences we might note if we visited nursing homes from conservative societies as opposed to those from more liberal ones. Visiting homes for the aged also help us prepare for other encounters in Israeli society and the broader world, including encounters with different languages and cultures.

As educators, we need to change the way we think about *Tikkun Olam* activities. It is important that we also think about *tikkun* of the person participating and the inherent opportunity to get to know the 'other' from a place of partnership and responsibility.

Learning About the World During Special Events

During the World Cup Soccer Tournament, a popular event for sports lovers that is held every four years, many teenagers, as well as parents and educators, take part in the viewing experience. When the World Cup is hosted on our side of the world, students skip classes to watch games. When it is on the other side of the world, they arrive to class utterly exhausted from watching all night. As someone who is interested in the game, I fully understand them. The event touches on an interest in sports as well as curiosity about world geography. When I was a child, I recall that Israeli banks would hand out a board game; on the upper side was a flag with a makeshift window underneath it. When you slid the window open, it showed which country the flag belonged to and what its capital city was. There is nothing like the World Cup for teaching about continents, countries, flags and capitals. The same idea can be implemented with the Eurovision Song Contest—a European event that is popular in Israel, the Olympics or any other international event.

To 'Plant' the World in Earth

Classroom walls and hallways are great spaces to create an environment that arouses curiosity and expands the students' horizons. The map of one's home country and the map of the world may be a mere background picture, but if the teacher asks every student to show him a city or country map mentioned in the news, the teacher will be helping to 'plant' the world in the person. This is also true regarding children's rooms at home. In one of the Village Way communities, a map of the world was put up in the hallway and staff marked with a pin and thread where each community member came from. The team adopted this idea following a tour of a traveling exhibition at a museum. The highlighted map created fascinating conversational opportunities. A creative educator in another community added a permanent corner on a bulletin board called 'Did you know?' She posted interesting facts to spark curiosity and inspire people to ask where to look for answers.

From *Tikkun HaLev* to *Tikkun Olam* at the Passover Seder

Every year before Passover, people begin to ask: "Where are you going to be for the seder?" For many, the holidays provide an inherent emotional and social safety net. It is not for nothing that Bruno Bettelheim in his book *A Good Enough Parent* referred to holidays as the "secret days of the heart."[33] A child or teenager who returns to a holiday table full of family and friends inadvertently turns this into his safety net. These are the people who will be by his side in moments of joy and moments of crisis. For those of our students without a family, holidays may instead be the 'open days of pain.' It is almost always possible to spend the holiday with a host family, to travel to friends or stay at the Village, but all these options mainly highlight the absence of family. Students are often concerned with how they are perceived by friends. There have been some cases of students at youth villages who stay in the village for the weekend, but nevertheless pack a bag and board a train with everyone. Once at the central bus station, they turn around and return to the village, so ashamed are they to be seen as having no one.

---

33   Bruno Bettelheim. *A Good Enough Parent: A Book on Child-Rearing*, Knopf, 1987

I remember a quarrel between two girls born in Ukraine. One of them, a member of a program for teens who immigrate to Israel without their families (their parents often follow later) had no family in Israel, while the other girl had no family at all. The conflict began around a cleaning shift in the dining hall on a holiday eve and deteriorated into a painful conversation. The first girl said: "No wonder you are so selfish. You don't have any family in this world, and because of that, you do not take others into consideration." The second student answered bitterly: "My mother died. That is why I am here. It's better than a mother who throws her child away to live in another country and does not care about her at all." Two harsh, hurtful statements reflected the pain that a holiday without a family may engender.

At Yemin Orde, we had invested a lot of time and thought into creating a warm atmosphere for Shabbat and the holidays. From family-style seating in the dining room to traditional home-cooked food to active conversations and hosting graduates and other interesting people—it was all part of the plan. All of this had an impact on the atmosphere of the holiday, but there was a feeling that something was missing. Although these preparations certainly made the stay pleasant for those who had nowhere to be for the holiday, many still left the holiday table with an empty feeling.

A significant change in the atmosphere during holidays and vacation days occurred when we began to host bereaved families. We managed to create such a unique atmosphere that the students stayed with us for the holiday, not because they had nowhere to go, but because we needed them to entertain these families. And so, in preparation for the Passover holiday, we were able show all the students at the Village the hardships of bereaved families, and how to make it easier for them. We approached the kids who wanted to volunteer and be included in the hospitality team. We also asked the bereaved families to join us in creating a family holiday atmosphere, in order to ease the situation for the kids without a family to return home to. On the eve of the Passover seder, in which all celebrants became symbolically free, the bereaved families joined with those with no family to develop emotional resilience as well as a sense of social responsibility and belonging.

It is the circular movement between *Tikkun HaLev* and *Tikkun Olam* that drives a person and symbolizes the endless progress that is the essence of life. Work on the self leads to the constant striving for a healthy society, which in turn, spurs a life of meaning. The circle is infinite and represents the growth process over the course of our lives.

There is a symbiotic relationship between the two circles. The individual affects the society, much as society affects the individual. Through *tikkun*, humanity and the world grow simultaneously. The circles have the power to propel our entire educational philosophy and help to move us forward in every aspect of education. The constant striving enables all elements to be carried out in full force.

Efforts to strengthen both *Tikkun HaLev* and *Tikkun Olam* can help us address communal distress in various places in the world. By helping people strengthen themselves individually, as well as teaching them to help the 'other,' we can break the cycle of competitive, survival-based living. At times, traumatized people who had to struggle to survive may feel it is legitimate to exploit others for personal advantage. By helping such people move into an empowered mindset, identifying the needs of and learning to accept the 'other,' we can have a real societal impact.

It Takes a Whole Village to Raise a Child

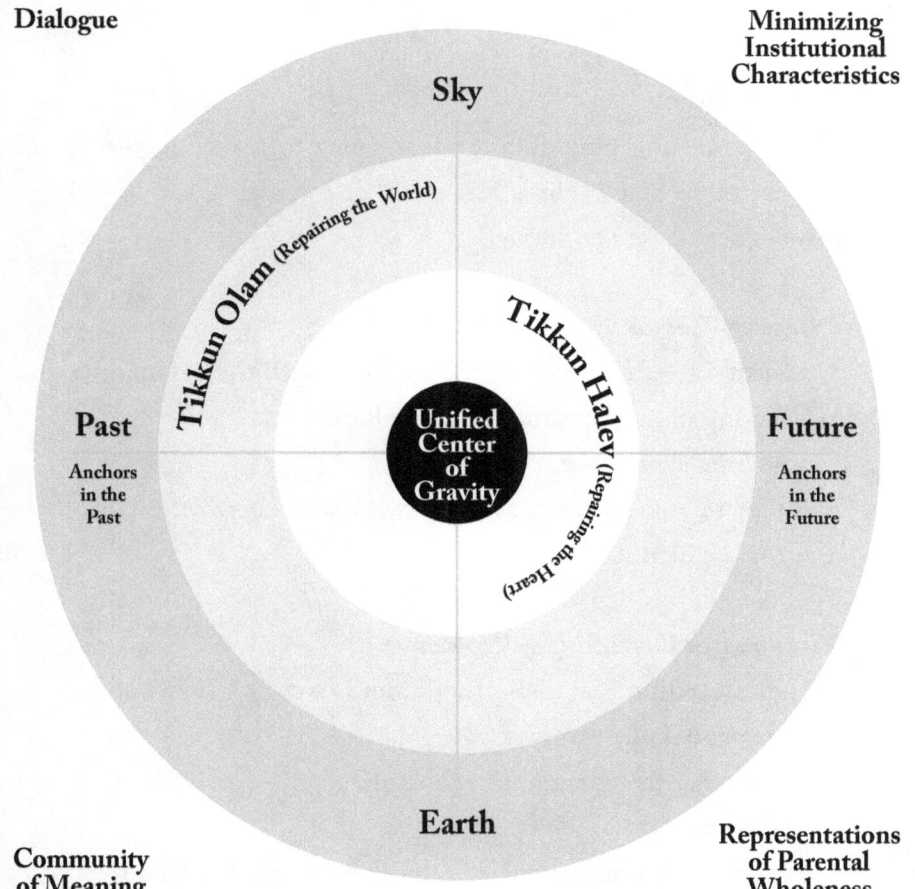

Core Principles of *Tikkun HaLev*

A Person Repairs the World and the World Repairs the Person.

Tikkun HaLev

Through setting boundaries, the essence of the educational process takes place. The *Tikkun HaLev* (repairing the heart) process occurs on two levels:

Ongoing *Tikkun*:
- Identifying strengths and sharing them with the community
- Creating more opportunities for ethical, social, and academic experiences of success
- Reflecting on experiences of success and their effect on future challenges

Tikkun after Disciplinary Problems:
- Understanding that disrupting order is a cry for help and an **educational opportunity**
- Identifying the communal **values** affected by the violation of the rule
- Educational responses that promote **principled behavior**

Three Elements of Tikkun HaLev:
- **Experiences of Success:** Opportunities for social, ethical, and academic success that are provided within the context of community life
- **Emotional Resilience:** The byproduct of empowering students with advancement programs, group therapeutic sessions and individual guidance

- **Tikkun Process:** A system by which the community creates a dialogue and a plan of action that leads to progress after moments of communal crisis

Core Principles of *Tikkun Olam*

The World Repairs a Person and the Person Repairs the World

Tikkun Olam

Tikkun Olam (repairing the world) expresses our commitment to a lifestyle of giving and a sense of responsibility for the community. An active effort to transcend one's own world and benefit others is essential for the growth of a person. Educators need to create opportunities in which the student moves from the mindset of a survivor to a leader. The survivor is a person who takes so he can exist, while the leader both gives and receives so that he can sustain others. Expanding the knowledge base and emotional horizons of adolescents together with offering opportunities to give to the 'other' will enable young people to end the cycle of societal distress and break their personal glass ceilings.

Three Elements of Tikkun Olam:

- **Giving, Commitment, and Responsibility:** Educating toward a sense of responsibility, involvement and giving at the individual and group levels
- **Communal Awareness of *Tikkun Olam*: A community of meaning** that is committed to caring for and empowering the good in its immediate surroundings and in expanding circles
- **To Plant the World in the Person:** Expanding horizons and instilling curiosity and knowledge in a way that moves across cultures

CHAPTER 4

The Corners of the Educational Field

In dwelling, live close to the ground—
Heart, should be open; contact with others, requires gentleness and
grace; partnership,
is first of all loyalty (trustworthiness);
When there is order you do not need laws; in order to succeed, you
need to use thought; every movement requires its own right moment.
—When you do not complain, the essence is revealed, not the flaws
　　　　　　　　　　　　　　　　　　　　　　　　—Lao Tzu[34]

Systematic Failures—What to do?

By its very nature, the educational field is complex and dynamic, offering sometimes contradictory messages. There are various aspects to contend with: educators and students, varied learning frameworks, educational values and the development of social, emotional and life skills. We seek to transform our educational community into one based upon three premises: a community that functions as a 'whole village,' a community in which the adults are meaningful educators for the children and a community in which each person has a significant place. As we work toward that goal, we encounter bureaucracy, alienating language and constant conflict between students, parents, and staff. We face challenges, opportunities and conflicts that are inherent in the educational field.

---

34   Lao Tzu, "Advice for Being on Your Way" *The Book of Tau,* Hebrew *translation(* Even Choshen, 2002)

We chose to mark these opportunities at 'four corners' of the graphic depiction which we call: **minimizing institutional characteristics, reliable representations of parental wholeness, dialogue, and community of meaning.**

Our ultimate goal is to maintain what we call a 'community of meaning,' where each member feels a sense of belonging. We facilitate the place of the individual in the community as one who can express himself through 'dialogue.' Additionally, adults in the community are present for young people; they are authentic, confident and professional. Adults must represent and occasionally even assume the role of parents. All of this occurs in an educational framework in addition to the required curriculum, ceremonies, grades, and other aspects.

To a certain extent, the 'four corners' of the Village Way roadmap represent both the challenge and the goal. When we know how to act harmoniously with and through them, the educational field functions as a meaningful community. In this community, educators work on the 'timeline' through 'anchors in the past and in the future' in educational environments that connect 'earth' and 'sky' and offer opportunities for individual and communal *tikkun*.

Minimizing Institutional Characteristics

Hello, customer service, it's me speaking,
Yes, may I help you?
I'm sorry ma'am, I know you've waited a long time in the queue
* no; I cannot transfer you to my supervisor*
ma'am, protocol talks here: contracts, performance reviews,
bonuses for outstanding human resources,
and on the first of the month, a cheque that doesn't quite cover the
roots of gray hair.
(Ma'am, can't you hear your baby is crying?)

                    —*It's Me Speaking*, Yudit Shahar, Israeli poet[35]

---

35   Yudit Shahar, It's Me Speaking [*Zu Ani Medaberet*] (Tel Aviv: Babel, Mishkal, Yediot Aharonot and Sifray Hemed, 2009), translated by Lauren Gordon, 2012 in poetryinternational.org

Every adolescent is entitled to, and deserves to, form his own personal identity, including a moral position, in relation to his family and other adults in his natural community, rather than in relation to an institution. Every adolescent is entitled to a close relationship with a supportive adult in which the adult authentically cares and feels responsible for the success of the adolescent, not just because it is his job.

What happens when life does not work out that way, and children or adolescents are educated primarily in institutions, subsequently identifying the teacher, educator, or informal educator as a key figure in forming their identity? These adolescents may form their identity in relation to the institution rather than the family, and the institution must say to itself: We are aware that we are an institution, but in order for the adolescent to go through the best possible process, we need to be as un-institutional as possible.

An educational community that seeks to operate as a unified community of meaning that impacts both the educators and students within it must minimize its institutional characteristics. It is important to adjust that which may be conceived as cold and alienating, such as forms, schedules or waiting in line. In the case of youth villages where students live on the premises, attention should also be paid to type of dishes and bedding used, or how allowance is distributed. It is important to make such places warmer and more familial and to maintain the supportive personal relationships within them.

At the same time, we need to recall that despite all the effort, the educational community will always remain an institution. We, therefore, propose that the institutional characteristics be minimized, not eliminated. It is important that the level of minimization match the development stage of the adolescent. Sometimes, institutional characteristics serve as preparation for life, such as military service or the working world, where the adolescent will encounter institutional life and have to adapt to the situation. There is no need to create an institutional setting for this purpose; however, we should not panic when engaging some institutional elements. They are an important part of life, and they have a purpose. The minimization of institutional characteristics is manifested in two ways: in shaping the physical environment of the educational community and in the quality of the interpersonal relationship between the staff and the young people.

Minimizing Institutional Characteristics in Designing the Environment

The educational environment should be designed in a way that is as close as possible to a home. We must shape the environment in a way that conveys warmth and belonging, and that preserves practical elements. Furniture for the students' homes and classrooms, curtains and clocks in the classroom, flower pots and scented soaps in the bathroom, background music during recess, safe and comfortable refreshment corners for the students, comfortable sofas and chairs that convey a homelike atmosphere in public spaces—all of these contribute to a corrective experience for adolescents who have felt alienated from the establishment and the educational institutions they have previously attended.

Minimizing Institutional Characteristics in Interpersonal Relationships

Interpersonal relationships between staff members and teens should be based both on the adult's role as an educator as well as their humanity, outside of a defined role. The history teacher may be an adult who just imparts knowledge—one that treats the student as a receptacle that must be filled with the knowledge required to pass the test—and if so, the relationship between the educator and the student will be purely functional and institutional. The same teacher, however, can simultaneously educate about history *and* view teaching as an opportunity for a human encounter, so the learning material becomes an opportunity for discourse on values. Thus, the adolescent may choose that teacher as the supportive adult on whom he can rely during the challenging stage of adolescence and beyond.

A relationship requires time to develop. Students often find it difficult to believe that what motivates the educator is caring and believing in them. Sometimes, at home as well, adolescents suspect their parents care what the surrounding environment thinks about their parenting more than they care about the child himself. Children and teens recognize insincerity and sometimes suspect it despite the presence of an adult who does authentically care. Many young people find it hard to believe that anyone cares about them. It takes a long process to build a meaningful relationship based on mutual respect.

Building trust is our responsibility. As adults, we carry the "burden of proof." If a teenager does not trust the adult world and believes that the educator expects him to get up in the morning and function because: "This is his job and that's why they pay him a salary ... and he doesn't care about me," we need to prove to him that there are other factors in the equation. After all, the kid is right. We are indeed getting paid, but we will never succeed if that is the only thing that drives us. Even as parents, we may hear our teen claim that we are involved because: "It's your job as parents." We need to prove to young people that we make demands because we care, are responsible for them, and maybe even love them, and not only due to the role society has assigned to us or in order to earn a salary. However, despite this crossing over into personal warmth, we must refuse to relinquish principles and important institutional rules. We try to prove that we are not a part of an ordinary institution. It is difficult to prove what we are **not** something, but we can certainly prove that we **are** caring and willing to go beyond the task for which we are paid. In this way, over time, the young person will feel they belong to the community beyond the framework of its institutions. Take Yuval's story, for example.

Yuval missed a lot of school. We had a conversation to understand the reason for these absences, and it turned out that his mother, who lived near Yemin Orde, had serious back problems and needed her son to accompany her to the doctor. She could not get to her treatments because the clinic was far from home and she found it difficult to use public transportation (and therefore never came to the family days at the Village). In a phone conversation with a friend from the neighborhood, we were able to make an appointment with a doctor and make sure that there would be someone to drive her and Yuval, and wait for them outside to take them home afterward. Our social network enabled us to do this with little effort. This small act established Yuval's trust in an educator who went above and beyond what was required of him.

A genuine interest in the well-being of a student's family, or for example, remembering a personal detail such as a pet's name, are symbolic acts that sow the seeds of trust, which will grow into a sincere, caring relationship. The educational community has a duty to do everything possible to help its students grow. It is part of an ongoing *tikkun* process and the desire for excellence, doing our best and constantly advancing. At the same time, it is important that we recognize the limits of our ability and authority. Out of the yearning for a meaningful, caring, and non-institutional relationship with students, we may feel responsible for tragic and unfortunate situations. While this kind of introspection, self-reflection and even criticism is vital in the *tikkun* process, there are situations we cannot fix due to countless factors. The tension between our sense of responsibility and humility is not easy, and occasionally, the line becomes blurred:

Dina, a 9th grader, immigrated to Israel without her parents three years prior to coming to Yemin Orde, at first living with an aunt in a situation that was less than ideal. She came to us as a survivor. She had numerous emotional and material difficulties and was unprepared for studies and other life challenges, but still she pressed on. Her difficult story inspired a lot of empathy and led us to try to help her and be by her side. Dina threatened suicide several times and was treated accordingly by professionals. In one incident, there was doubt as to whether she had tried to hurt herself, so a professional referred her to the ER of a mental hospital. She went there with a Village educator and I arrived as quickly as possible. I asked the informal educator to return to the group and I stayed with Dina.

After an hour of apprehension, the psychiatrist on call decided to hospitalize her. Dina objected, and I was asked by the psychiatrist to sign the hospitalization permit. I replied that I was not the guardian and therefore had no authority to do so, but that I would like to hear the basis for his decision. After offering an explanation that did not convince me, the psychiatrist was forced to recruit signatures from two more doctors. In the meantime, I contacted the director of the Village and told him I would not leave Dina alone for even a minute. He said we seemed to have no other option but to follow the doctor's recommendation, and he hung up. Thus, the decision was made for forced hospitalization in the closed ward. Dina began to cry and shout: "Don't let them put me in a madhouse. They'll poison me with drugs; don't leave me!" She held on tight to me. I could not and did not want to leave her. I called the Village director again, and asked him: "If, Heaven forbid, it was your daughter, what would you do?" He replied: "I think I would take a long vacation from work and stay close to her with proper professional care." I told him I was asking for a week's leave to stay with her. When the director arrived, he refused to grant me the vacation because he said he could not leave 50 staff members and 450 children without a director of informal education because of one kid. It was hard to accept, but we acknowledged that as much as we cared, we were not really her parents. Dina was hospitalized for two exceptionally long weeks. We were with her every evening, according to the therapist's instructions, and she returned to the educational community with very mixed feelings. At the end of the year, she left and severed contact with us.

Both educators and parents deal with the broadest range of serious issues that life has to offer. We need to be present for the students as well as our own children. At the same time, we must humbly recognize our own limitations and be aware that the child himself, his fate, his environment and life itself have their own say in the outcome.

The term 'minimizing institutional characteristics' refers to the attempt by an educational community to recognize the fact that it is an institution, and at the same time, wishes to reduce the cold and alienating elements as much as possible. We recognize we are neither home nor parents, yet we strive to complement parental authority and be the closest thing, without standing in the way of their parents.

Reliable Representations of Parental Wholeness

The presence of parental figures is necessary for young people. Their rebellion and shows of independence by teens may make us think that this is not the case, but specifically during adolescence, kids are in constant need of a stable, accepting, and boundary-setting adult to help them understand both the world and themselves. Educational activity can be a means to reinforce the connection between an educator and a child. That connection, in turn, shapes the methods of discourse, learning and daily life. Such a presence can exist only when the educator acts in an authentic way and is aware of the importance of his role.

As educators, we must remember that our role is to be supportive adults, not parents. We cannot really replace parents, and it is important not to pretend we can. The best parenting is supposed to provide every child with fertile ground for growth and development, allowing them to absorb lessons and be nurtured through their families to shape their personalities.

- **Material Sustenance:** As described by psychologist Abraham Maslow in his Hierarchy of Needs, a person has existential needs such as the need for food, clothing, and a place to sleep. A student who does not eat well does not learn well. The presence of a student who has not changed his shirt for a week, whether from a lack of awareness of hygiene or from material lack, should immediately trigger an informed response from a supportive adult. That response may be embarrassing to adolescents, but it is a necessary element in the representation of optimal parenting. Much of the students' difficulty in applying themselves to learning and the search for meaning derives from deprivation, and we must try to help. It is impossible to fix everything, but one can certainly express caring and take steps to help fulfill material needs.

- **Emotional Sustenance:** A person develops emotional resilience in accordance with the experiences to which he is exposed. When I saw how my father coped with the death of my grandfather, I learned that it was okay for adults to feel sad and to express pain. In my parents' home, I was exposed to the processing of emotions in situations of joy, pain, and crisis. These observations entered my life and formed my own emotional resilience. The ability to cope is not a luxury but an existential need, and a supportive educator should be aware that part of his role is to enable the teen to develop such resilience. When teenagers do not have a supportive adult with whom they can share challenges and emotional issues, it is important to create opportunities for young people to share their experiences through individual or group discussions with their peers.

- **Modeling Values:** A teenager growing up in a supportive home absorbs values from his daily life without the need for workshops and training. For example, he sees that his parents are active in animal rights organizations, or that at every community event, they are the first to participate and take responsibility for organizing. On the other hand, a young person exposed to negative actions will absorb the values behind them and learn to act accordingly. An adult must remember that he is an ethical role model for adolescents. They see a lot more than we think.

They watch all the time. We need to be aware of this and allow them to experience our ethical behavior, including that which is not related to our official role.

During my time as an educator at Yemin Orde, my family's house was in the middle of the Village, right on the walking path from the high school to the dining hall. In one of the classes, I heard a fight between students regarding male and female roles in the household. Many felt that cleaning and cooking were "women's work." I looked for a way to send a different message without coming out and saying it directly. I therefore chose to do the chore of hanging our laundry on the line during the school lunch period. These kinds of simple acts can have a ripple effect on teenagers. They become accustomed to seeing new options for ways to behave in the world, which can shape their values.

Focusing on being a stable force may help us diagnose signs of distress in students. We can ask: What bothers him at this moment? What does not allow him to function? Is it material, ethical or emotional sustenance? Clearly, material sustenance affects emotional resilience and ethical behavior, and vice versa. An educator who notices that a boy needs glasses and helps him through solutions that the system can offer is responding to a physical need that may have a tremendous effect on the self-confidence, emotional strength, and even the ethical behavior of that boy.

Strengthening the Relationship between Parents and Teenagers

As we try to make up for what is missing in adolescents' lives by taking a complementary approach to the parental role, we may be the ones who end up weakening the authority held by the students' parents. The better the educator is, the more likely he is to take the place of the parent, especially when it comes to parents from disadvantaged backgrounds—although, in a sense, all parents of teens are perceived by the adolescent as irrelevant at times. For their part, parents often find themselves unsatisfied with the choices made by their adolescent children. So, what do we do as educators? We certainly do not become mediocre to make space for a parent. Teens deserve the best and we as educators are committed to doing the best for them. However, we must understand that part of our educational mission is to strengthen the connection between children and their parents in two central ways: empowering the adolescent in the eyes of his parents and empowering the parents in the eyes of the adolescent.

An example of a small step that works towards this goal is to add their parents' names on the certificates of excellence given to students. No extra effort is required of the educator, and the young person who receives such a certificate understands that the educator appreciates his efforts and attributes them to the student's parents and family as well. Parents that receive such a certificate understand that the educator respects all the days and nights they invested in the child. Teens' appreciation of their parents' wisdom, love and caring is necessary for the success of the entire educational process.

No Substitute for Parents

What happens when teachers don't see these admirable characteristics in their students' parents? The answer is that he must work hard to search for them. Only in rare cases is it impossible to find positive qualities in parents. It is more common for educators to devote themselves to the fantasy of "saving this child from his parents," which is not right for the child and not good for the process. A good educator is committed to professional humility that will enable him to see good in every person, even when it is concealed from view. Of course, there are also cases of abusive parents that require treatment from appropriate professionals.

Strengthening the Relationship Between Parents and Educators

There is a lot of talk about the importance of the relationship between teachers and parents, but there is a tendency to underestimate the importance of parents when they are from a disadvantaged background. Educators may think: "After all, they are struggling in their own lives, why should we involve them?" This attitude may belie a lack of consideration or appreciation, as if to say: "What do they understand? They will only interfere." But the importance of communicating with parents, no matter what their life circumstances, remains essential to the entire educational process.

The relationship with parents takes place in three areas: in the educational community (parents meetings/parent-teacher conferences, family day, informal meetings to discuss issues that arise); in the students' home (home visits/house calls), and with ongoing communication (emails, contact sheets, phone calls, text messages). To properly utilize these resources, we must return to the central question: Why is contact with parents so important? In the parent-teacher-child triangle, the most important side of the triangle connects the child to the parent. If you want to foster growth among adolescents, you need to allow them an experience of cohesion where they, their parents and their educators walk hand in hand. Goals of contact with parents include:

- Creating a partnership between educators and parents
- Strengthening the bond between parents and teens through mutual empowerment
- Strengthening the connection between educators and students

Parent Days and Parent-Teacher Conferences

At parent meetings, we host our students' parents on campus, and it is important to invest in hospitality. The meeting is not only for reporting on grades and behavior but also offers a key opportunity for parents to voice their insights, ask questions, and make suggestions. This is a chance to empower the child in front of their parents and share experiences of success—whether the young person can sing well or play an instrument; whether they painted a portrait or wrote an essay that can be displayed in a place of honor. It is important to create positive experiences for all.

In one educational community, a photographer made magnets for all the participants, so that every teen had a souvenir of a picture with his parents.

But what about the students whose parents do not come to the event? Many of the adolescents do not want their parents to come, and then it is important to explain the event to the child and include him in the process. If the young people realize this is an event to honor their parents, they are more likely to ask parents to come. If the students have a platform to present something of their own, it will be important to them that their parents be present, and they will take care to encourage them to come. When you create an atmosphere that is considerate, arranging transportation and investing in a personal invitation sent from the educator, the students try harder and more parents show up. And what about those who are still missing? In such situations, the student may be invited to choose supportive adults from the educational community who will attend. The chosen adult should be sensitive in accepting the compliment of being chosen, but at the same time know his place, and after the event, offer to share the experience with the parent. There may be parts of the event that the student must participate in alone, and then the educator or student may update the parents after. The option to change the accepted name from "Parents' Day" to "Family Day" is for the benefit of those whose parents cannot attend for various reasons, allowing them to feel part of that day.

When Do We Invite Parents?

Another opportunity in which we host parents is following a disciplinary problem, a return from suspension or a wake-up call that asks: "Where do we go from here?" The parents' invitation is perceived by the student as a punishment. It may be uncomfortable for the student to ask his parents to change their schedules to come or he may feel ashamed of himself. There are educators who reinforce this perception and add threats such as "I will report to your parents" or "Next time, I will invite your parents." Parents are not a punishment. The purpose of inviting them is to share the details of the situation and to make a decision regarding next steps in order to make a collective decision even though a decision will ultimately be in the hands of the parents or the educational staff.

Inviting parents does not have to happen in relation to a negative event. But let us try to recall how many times we as educators invite the parents of teenagers because of a positive event such as a leading role in a performance, receiving a certificate of excellence, or completing a challenging hike. We should do this more often. Since this is a partnership, we need to create a good feeling, and positive experiences can contribute to it.

At the technological school in Daliyat al-Carmel, a Druze Heritage Week was held, including a variety of activities inspired by previous conversations with their parents. The highlight of the week was an exhibition of the students' work and a traditional singing performance in the presence of the parents and dignitaries of the community. I wandered among the pictures taken by the boys and met an elderly man whose clothes and mustache indicated that he was religious and one of the dignitaries of the community. We said hello to each other, and I tried to initiate a conversation. I introduced myself and so did he, and I asked if his son was attending school. He answered softly, as if ashamed: "What can I do? I have a son who went to high school in Haifa and is now studying medicine, and I have a daughter who is a student at the University, and then, well, there is also the one who is studying here." I was surprised by his answer, which conveyed a lack of regard for his son. I told him that the school was a good one and I turned his attention to the impressive exhibition. But in the end, he said: "Every family has a black sheep." I was pained for the child, that this was the message he received from his father, and I felt pain for the father who was influenced by social pressures according to which the success of his children's education has only one path—through the halls of academia. All he wanted was for this son to follow in the footsteps of his brother, the doctor, but instead, the young man was attending a vocational high school. Just then, the boy approached his father, hugged him and invited him to see his work. After the exhibition, the show began. I recognized the man's son on stage as he began to sing in Arabic in a pleasant, moving voice. The audience was moved with him. I went up to the father and said: "Your son sings like an angel. He sings beautifully." He replied: "True, it's not bad." After a few minutes, one of the educators went up to the father and whispered in his ear. He seemed reluctant, but she begged again and pleaded, and finally, he agreed. He went on stage with a darbuka (Middle Eastern drum) and accompanied his son who was singing. The educators who knew of the fraught father-son relationship applauded with enthusiasm. It was hard not to get excited watching the father see his son in a position of strength. And there was his father, showing respect for his son in front of everyone by joining him in the music.

Home Visits: An Opportunity

The home visit is an opportunity both to strengthen the child and the relationship between the child and his family. This is an opportunity to meet the parents in their comfort zone and allow them to host us. During such a visit, we should be guests first, learning about the rules and traditions and enjoying the moment. Then, we can slowly learn more about where the child grew up, the atmosphere and the conditions. A large picture of someone in the living room may be a key to understanding one behavior or another. Listening to a story about a student's childhood told by his parents can help us to create a channel for good communication in the future. As with every opportunity, there is the potential risk that visiting the home will weaken relations, instead of strengthening them. In contrast to the events in which we host the parents, we are the guests. I emphasize this because I have encountered educators and therapists who acted as if they were the hosts, even while visiting someone else's home. A home visit reporting form is essential for good order, but it is important not to fill it out during the visit. All critical data should be absorbed in a positive, non-technical way, not as if this were a security investigation. We do not criticize the house or the parents; we simply visit.

Ongoing Communication

Digital media allows us to transmit important information to students and parents, and vice versa. It is much easier and faster to send a written message than to make a call, so it is appropriate to use this media. A message does not replace every phone call, just as a telephone call does not replace every face-to-face meeting. Nevertheless, the group messages on the popular app WhatsApp facilitate group communication. It is appropriate to use this kind of app for short, important messages to update the parents and to help them share successes. It is also helpful to use an app like WhatsApp to establish one-on-one contact with parents and to help them in a way that reflect their interests and strengths.

We still live in a reality where when a parent receives a message or phone call from a teacher, he or she often responds defensively or in a panic. In one of our *batei midrash* (a learning session for senior staff), we asked the team to describe their relationships with their students' parents. All of them reflected a bleak situation in which the relationship with the parents was based on disciplinary problems. Two weeks later, the principal announced the need for positive weekly communication with parents. Every week, they were to have two positive conversations on the phone without any mention of disciplinary problems. A decision was later made by management that all initial contact with parents must be positive, so that a staff member who wants to involve parents in dealing with a disciplinary problem must first carry out a positive introductory conversation.

I'm Not Their Mother

One of the complaints of the Israelites in the wilderness caused Moses to stand before G-d and complain: "Did I conceive all these people, did I bear them?"[36] Moses makes clear that he is not the people's mother and cannot take on total responsibility for them. G-d's answer to Moses is to gather 70 men of the elders of Israel to assist him. According to the

---

36   Numbers 11:12, JPS

Biblical story, even a leader like Moses cannot do his work alone. He needs a 'whole village.'

While parents are responsible for the needs of their children, the educator in the community is not solely responsible. Each community also has extensive staff and resources for offering psychological counseling. The relationship between the educator and the student symbolizes the entire educational community. The supportive adult represents the community for the child. Every teenager needs the presence of an adult who outlines a path. The supportive adult is an 'anchor' for him.

As educators, we must be authentic in our being—our values, beliefs, life experience and everything that makes us who we are. There is no technical method or instruction manual that can make our presence authentic. The most important resource is being who we really are, a three-dimensional educator. We need to be available to the children with our entire being. Contrary to the conventional advice: "Do not show them that you're hurt because they will take advantage of it," we try not to fear, and to say honestly that we were hurt because that, too, is a human dimension they must recognize. The tools help us to be present, but we cannot employ them without presenting our true selves.

The educator goes through a meaningful process. He grows with the educational process. His authenticity develops, connects him to himself, the student, the community and the entire educational endeavor. This is just like a parent who grows in his parental role as his child grows. An educator who is connected to himself and his feelings, and acts authentically, will go through a meaningful process with his students. Vered, a mathematics educator, talks about the process she went through:

> *It took time for me to understand the essence of my role as a meaningful presence for the youth during a significant period of their lives, and how this would enable them to find themselves. When I first started in my position, I was engaged in my students' scholastic achievement and their success in matriculation exams. Today, I feel that I allow*

myself to be there beyond the mission of teaching. I feel responsible for the broad educational process. The connections and conversations with the students have become ongoing and meaningful. Of course, I still insist on success on tests, but my insistence is a part of my caring and responsibility as a supportive adult in their lives. Over time, my belief in my own abilities to help and support them, as they believe in themselves, has grown. More and more, I realize that everything we do with the students in in the classrooms, and beyond, has a profound connection to their preparation for life.

Being an educator means understanding that the thoroughly human encounter between a supportive adult and an adolescent offers the opportunity for a deep bond that influences both parties. The mathematics *teacher* teaches equations without revealing her real personality to the students, while the mathematics *educator* understands the importance of a personal encounter that may help a teenager develop curiosity in the subject matter while also helping him find meaning in life.

Every adult in the educational community is a 'supportive adult and educator' even if he is not formally defined as such. Students often find a common language and are deeply influenced by the community administration and household staff. This was the case with Shlomo, who worked in maintenance in one of the educational communities:

Shlomo told us he was disappointed that on Yom Hazikaron, Israel's Memorial Day, some of the students would not attend the ceremony because they headed to the beach early to save their spot for Independence Day, which falls on the day after Memorial Day. Shlomo approached the school principal and said that such a situation was contrary to the values of the community and his personal values. He decided to try to recruit the students to join him in the Memorial Day custom he has held for years, to distribute water bottles to the bereaved families visiting their loved ones at military cemeteries. He spoke to the students and managed to recruit a group to volunteer on Memorial Day. This activity was so significant for the community that it became a longstanding tradition in the school.

Dialogue

"When you are in psychological distress
and someone really hears you
without passing judgement on you,
without trying to take responsibility for you,
without trying to mold you,
it feels damn good!"

—Carl Rogers[37]

Dialogue in its deepest sense allows everyone equal space and autonomy to formulate their personality and beliefs. Dialogue touches on the 'anchors of the timeline,' the routine of life on the 'spaceline,' and the *tikkun* processes. We must allow ourselves as adults to be present, to allow the students to see us and to know us while maintaining boundaries. We do this in accordance with the needs and abilities of the teen, allowing a space for independent development even if this is fundamentally different from the way we ourselves would lead him.

An authentic three-dimensional educator is one who expresses his feelings in daily situations, whatever he is feeling, whether angry, excited, happy or proud. His connection with students is sincere in a fundamental sense. This does not mean an uncontrolled burst of emotions, but that all interaction with students is conducted authentically and honestly. A three-dimensional educator recognizes his shortcomings and allows students to know about them.

---

37 Carl R. Rogers, *A Way of Being*. (Boston: Houghton Mifflin), 1980.

Not a Special Power

A real dialogue takes place between equals. An educational community is made up of people who are all equal before the law but inhabiting different roles. Therefore, the dialogue between an educator and a student is not truly equal in every sense. The dialogue is influenced by the position represented by the student and the position represented by the educator. Both make their perspectives clear, but when the time comes, the decision will be made by those who must bear the responsibility—the educators. We educate within frameworks where the hierarchy is clear, like in a family.

One might say: "If there is no equality anyway, we can skip the dialogue." But this is not so. Since in a school—as in a family—adults hold the greater share of responsibility, dialogue should be maintained as a central value and tool of the educational process. Educators may also harbor the concern that expanding their familiarity with students may confuse them, make them think they are their friends, and then harm the process, the educator and ultimately the students themselves. While maintaining a healthy balance is important, our experience shows that some educators can establish a dialogue with their students, thereby fostering a safe, open space for growth.

Shaul arrived at my office for a one-on-one work meeting. He was a new informal educator, someone easy to talk to, with a sense of humor, who understood the importance of the mission and tried hard. The conversation opened with him providing an updated report on the status of his group and continued with him saying that he was really stuck on the topic of personal conversations with the students. He explained that he cleared 30 to 45 minutes for each individual student, and on many of these occasions, he did not know what to do with the time. The conversation felt forced, he said. "They don't really want it, don't cooperate or open up, and there are many long, embarrassing silences. "

Shaul and I have children who are the same age, and at that point, I changed the topic of conversation and moved on to speaking about how hard it was for me to set boundaries for my younger son, and how it affected the whole family. Shaul very much identified with this and immediately shared his own doubts and difficulties regarding his son. The conversation unfolded until suddenly Shaul smiled and said: "Oh, I get it, you're actually simulating a one-on-one conversation with me right now, aren't you?" Consciously or not, I wanted to illustrate to Shaul what happens in one-on-one conversations that makes them meaningful and intimate. As soon as I shared my own challenges, he inadvertently devoted himself to the conversation and shared a similar challenge. From there, the conversation unfolded naturally.

One-on-one conversations with teenagers require us to peel away the layers. In preparing for such a conversation, it is a good idea to think about something from your own story to share in a controlled manner, something that might allow the child to open up. One-on-one conversations allow you to devote time to the teenager, not because something unusual happened, but because the young person is important. As parents, we talk to our children a great deal along the way, and very rarely—if at all—do we devote time to a one-on-one conversation. This is an important gift for them and for us.

Field trips and activities that include breaking routine provide great opportunities for thoughtful dialogue. The different schedule and location make it possible to get to know each other from new perspectives. Often, the relationships deepen in informal settings. An open conversation ensues, an opportunity to see each other in another light, and then to express strengths, weaknesses and vulnerabilities. Many educators and students can attest to significant relationships that began outside of the usual framework. Often, we need to leave the formal framework to feel safe enough to expose our true selves. This authentic presence serves as a model for students. As we have said, sometimes even within the formal framework, we can bring something of ourselves. Miriam, an educator in one of the Village Way communities, talks about it:

158   DOTAN LEVI

I didn't like to talk about myself. I thought that it was not serious or appropriate. But after participating in one of the Village Way sessions, on the topic of The Three-Dimensional Educator, I felt that there was meaning to my sharing, that it could have a positive impact. I shared with the students, and I saw that it helped. For example, in one of my homeroom classes we dealt with the topic of goodbyes. I came to the class with a whole prepared lesson plan, but I felt that I must bring something of myself to the lesson. I shared with them a personal story about a difficult goodbye to my father who had died that year, how he had asked for forgiveness before his passing and how that was significant for me. I asked everyone to tell something personal about goodbyes. We used the Village Way concepts of the 'timeline,' 'anchors in the past and anchors in the future,' Tikkun HaLev and Tikkun Olam in addressing the issues of goodbyes. Very personal, meaningful stories came up, and the students did not want to leave the classroom. At the beginning of the class, I promised to release them at 1:20, and suddenly without us noticing, is was already a-quarter-to-two, and the secretaries called to remind us to leave because the buses had arrived. Until that day, I did not know that personal issues should be brought up. It has been a turning point in my role as an educator and has greatly influenced my class.

Spontaneous Dialogue in the Whole Village

The Village Way defines the word **dialogue** as a significant component in the lived routine of an educational village: the way the principal talks to the staff, the way the staff speak to one another, the way the teachers talk to the students, and certainly, the way the students talk to each other. A dialogue that lives and breathes the "I in Thou,"[38] as philosopher Martin Buber termed it, is a value-laden experience that helps teens grow up to be independent adults who contribute to the community.

---

38   Martin Buber, *I and Thou*, (New York: Scribner, 1958)

Dialogue is expressed in the language we choose, our intonation, and body language. The language adults choose affects the quality of the dialogue throughout the community, and, as mentioned in the first basic principle, a common language is created when people share a common purpose. The question is only whether it is a language of growth that creates positivity or a shallow language that lacks awareness of its own power to shape reality.

Dialogue is expressed in every interaction in our daily routine, in random encounters in the school hallways, on the sidewalk, during the lesson, in a sympathetic glance and in a smiling greeting which conveys, "I see you and it makes me smile." The quality of dialogue is tested in moments of crisis, in the *tikkun* process and when dealing with extreme situations.

Alongside spontaneous encounters, time for conversations must be set aside. True, we as educators already conduct such conversations, but as in the case of busy parents, our daily life is busy, and we usually end up talking about disciplinary problems or crises. Quite a few educators and parents have difficulty with personal conversations. They feel awkward and do not know how to manage the process. For their benefit and for the benefit of all, we have created several principles to help each educator have conversations with teens.

We Have All Been Children

During these conversations, we need to remember that we adults were all children in the past. This sentence can symbolize the two positions in which the educator must engage in a meaningful dialogue: to identify the 'I' in the 'other' (Buber's "Thou") without losing the self in the encounter.

We have all been children in the past. In every meaningful dialogue, we practice the vision of the "I in Thou," recalling the time we were children and teenagers. We try to understand the world of the teen from his point of view. Sometimes, you can play a role-playing game in which the teen assumes the role of the educator and vice versa. You can even switch chairs. This step may surprise the student and encourage refreshed thinking and conversation.

We have all been children **in the past.** The second stage in any meaningful dialogue requires the educator to remind himself and the student that although he was a child, he is now an adult with educational responsibility. I know of educators who became stuck in the role-playing game, identifying completely with the teen's pain and not making demands on him, or identifying with his anger and allowing him to think that violence might be legitimate. I once met a youth village informal educator who identified with a teenager who beat someone up when a fellow student had cursed him. In the staff room, the informal educator said: "I understand him. In fact, I would have reacted like that." While it is fair to be totally honest in a staff room, when in front of the child, the educator should return to the role of adult and reflect on the consequences of choosing violence. He can show understanding of the situation but disagree with the act. His job is to guide the young person to advance in his moral judgment.

Finding CALM in the Chaos

Dialogue is a meaningful part of getting to know the teenager and helping him to progress. We want to begin the situation by imparting a sense of calm, which is crucial when talking to teens, especially in the noisy, anxious rhythm of the teen years and of contemporary society. The word CALM also can help us to remember three important components of dialogue: communication, active listening, and putting ourselves on "mute."

Communication: Our communication needs to be adjusted to the pace, content, and length of the message that the adolescent is able to take in. In other words, the way we communicate must be in the 'radio frequency' that the adolescent receives. There are educators who speak AM when their students have long been on FM. It is not their fault. They are just not on the right frequency. So, the conversation should begin with "frequency calibration"—a few short, simple questions focusing on the facts, to make sure we are at the right frequency. When we fail to do this, the personal conversation can easily become a monologue by the educator performed in front of a young person with a glazed look, who is thinking: "What is with this guy? What does he want from me?"

It is important to remember that there are cases in which a red line has been crossed, and so the student has been called in for a disciplinary conversation mainly to listen and not for a fully participatory one-on-one conversation. However, even in such a conversation, the message should be clear and at the right frequency.

Active Listening: When conducting meaningful dialogue, we do not passively hear what is said, but actively listen. This can be seen in our body language through a look of curiosity and small gestures that show attention. For example, you could turn off your cellphone or silence it while explaining that you will only answer if there is something urgent. An important tool for active listening is reflecting. We listen to the teenager, and from time to time, we repeat in our own words what we understood from them: "You mean that ... so what you're actually telling me is that... " Students feel that we are listening and they can repeat their point until they think we have understood them.

Mute: An important part of the encounter is to pretend we are on a Zoom call, and 'put ourselves on mute,' allowing for a period of silence. We ask each person in the conversation to stay silent and we clear the room of all background noise. Silence in an interpersonal encounter allows for intimacy that can make one feel vulnerable, which usually provokes an impatient reaction from the adolescent, who may say something like: "So what?" It is important to encourage this kind of emotional vulnerability; for example, you might say: "I want to talk to you today about your plans for the future. I would like you to think about what you want to be when you grow up and whether what you are doing today is helping you in this direction. Before you answer, I ask that we be quiet for half a minute and think about things." As the bond becomes more secure, we can be more open, and the silence will not provoke the same level of resistance from the student.

The Boundaries of Tolerant Dialogue

A supportive adult authentically conveys the message of reciprocity and helps the student to bring something of himself to the conversation. She legitimizes difficulties, feelings and differences of opinion. A relationship based on dialogue sometimes involves confronting disagreements about fundamental beliefs, with the 'sky' of the educational community. We need to respect the student's autonomy and his heartfelt opinions. In one of my many conversations with Village Way founder Dr. Chaim Peri about the importance of educators tolerating students' nonconformist attitudes, he cited the story of a student called Sasha who decided—after learning the biblical story of the binding of Isaac—that he was not interested in any connection with Judaism.

> *Sasha, a boy who immigrated from Russia, taught me a lesson about the possibility of reinventing the meaning of "faith." For Sasha, exposure to the story of the binding of Isaac by Abraham—whom Jewish tradition sees as the first believer—was a terrible shock. Of all the stories he got to know at Yemin Orde, this biblical story shocked him. "I do not want to be part of a nation whose founding father was willing to kill his son," he said. In such situations, we must remind ourselves that every reaction of a young person is a legitimate response reflecting his feelings and thoughts at that moment, and that in years to come, he may add further interpretations. Sasha had many opportunities to express his opposition to religious beliefs and often declared himself an atheist. Despite what might be expected from educators in the religious Village at which he studied, his views were accepted calmly, without any opposition from the staff.*

The image of a father holding a knife to his son's neck is terrible. No wonder Sasha felt that this knife was also at his own neck! But his response also exposed the nature of the spiritual quest of adolescents, which we often struggle to understand. Sasha was unable to accept a story touching on the theme of human sacrifice, as such a fundamental threat may penetrate dramatically into the inner world of the adolescent. But Sasha's continuing opposition to the story also revealed a desire to shape his own identity. When adolescents challenge our teachings, it can seem like a desecration of the values that are most sacred to us. But, we must trust the internal emotional logic of our students, for this step is an attempt to create an ongoing dialogue with us, through which they will formulate their own way and clarify their piece of 'sky.'

Dialogue helps us develop our ability to make room for a multiplicity of opinions. Even when we aspire to educate according to our 'sky,' i.e. values and basic beliefs, it is important that we honor the autonomy of our students.

Community of Meaning

One afternoon, my family and I were hiking on the summit trail of Mount Meron, under the green cloak of oak trees. From time to time, a wide piece of landscape would appear, stretching out over the horizon in green curves. Afterward, we would go back into the trees whose silence charmed us. There was a great peace in this place and a kind of flower whose name I do not know, its deep blue accentuating the silence. I noticed that the oak trees on the southern slope were significantly higher than the oaks in the north. When I alerted my son to this, he added a note of his own that I had been thinking about for a long time. He said: "If the trees were wise, they would make an agreement between them to stay low. In the end, what they achieve when they struggle with each other for the light and everyone tries to grow higher could be achieved without fighting and without effort." I began to answer him something about the bushes that would struggle with the oaks, but after a moment I corrected myself and said, "But they do make an agreement!" "What agreement?" my son wondered. "In this agreement, every tree promises the other trees it will strive to challenge its neighbors, to encourage them to grow to their full glory, that it will not let them fall asleep in mediocrity." This remark made a great impression on my son. Then we continued to talk a bit about education."

—Dan Lasry, Israeli scholar of education
from *Pinocchio Goes Off the Rails.*[39]

As mentioned, humans have been community creatures since the dawn of mankind. By nature, we belong to many different communities. Every educational framework is a community that influences its members in one way or another. The discourse deals with significant issues in the students' world. The community paves a path for its members, helps them reach cohesion, and carries out significant *tikkun* processes. Every member of the community has their own place and a sense of belonging and pride in their association with it.

Who Are Members of The Community?

In one of the staff study sessions, which we call a *beit midrash*, we discussed our community membership. We placed each group within the community in a hexagon and tried to place all the hexagons in the form of a hive. The initial challenge went relatively easily. The list of community groups began with the students, the educators, the administration and the therapeutic staff, and ended with other partners such as security guards and the janitorial staff. We asked about whether parents should be part of the equation. At the end of a brief discussion, a decision was made. While

39   Dan Lasry. *Pinocchio Yored MahaPassim* [*Pinocchio Goes Off the Rails*] (Lior Sharf Publishers, 2004)

parents are in a meaningful interface with the community, they are not necessarily members of it. And what about the graduates? Graduates, the team members decided, must be considered part of the community.

We considered what made each group a part of the community and then examined the sense of belonging felt by each group. Which actions give one a place in the community? I shared that the more one gets involved and gives of him or herself, the more likely one is to experience belonging. Clearly, the educational staff felt a relatively deep sense of belonging because they were implementing the main purpose for which this community was founded—education. If so, what do the students do to earn their place in the community? After all, if they do not actively do something, they do not really belong. They may be the objects that generate meaning for adults, however, to feel part of the community, they must be partners within it too.

Is hard work enough to strengthen the sense of belonging to a community? Of course not. A staff member can work both day and night and still not feel a sense of meaning. And aside from monetary reward, the factor that most influences the quality of a staff member's work is the sense of meaning she experiences.

Service Provider or Partner in the Educational Process?

I visited Dana at her home. Now divorced with two lovely young girls, Dana finished her studies at Yemin Orde eight years earlier. Not surprisingly, the conversation turned to painful issues. Dana began to talk about the difficulty of raising girls alone, and her expectation that their father take responsibility and become more of a partner. When she spoke of the subject, she had a look of anger and pain on her face. It was dinner time, and while we were talking, Dana made a meal for her girls. I watched in amazement at the sharp transition she made when she served the girls the food. Her face lit up with a wide smile as she said, "Girls, here you go. Enjoy your meal." I could not resist asking, "How do you manage to transition so naturally?" She smiled and said simply: "I learned this from Azat, a staff member in the dining room of the Village. I remember one day when I was really upset. I came to the dining room with a grim face and stood in front of Azat, who was serving the main course. He looked at me like he did every day and could sense my feelings. He asked, "What's going on Dana? Smile!" "Leave me alone, I have no patience today" I answered him. Azat smiled, conveying a sense of understanding. He went into the storeroom, brought me a bag of chips and a lollipop, and said, "It's not so bad. Take this, and at least have a good rest of your day." I remember what that did for me, and even then, I thought to myself that when I become a mother, I will always try to serve my kids food with a smile on my face. I will look at them and try to see how they are feeling."

Azat is not only a dining room staff member who serves community members, he is a full-fledged member of the community and a significant partner in the educational process. But the question remains: How does he see himself, and how do other members of the community see him? Naturally, every community has members with different tasks and roles. There is a high probability that the community members who are support staff will be seen by the educational staff as service providers only, and this will certainly impact the students, even in relation to how they perceive themselves. But to be a member of a community of meaning is to understand that each member has a responsibility and a significant role in the educational process. This is not just a slogan designed to empower employees and encourage them to do better work. It is a way of life. It is a moral truth. To this end, support staff should be included in some professional training sessions and in some meetings with the educational staff to discuss educational and operational issues.

Involving the support staff requires that we understand the world that the children come from. The support staff often knows the world of the students better than the educational staff. They are also more approachable and are connected to students through gentler channels. The support staff knows that sometimes a meaningful word and a hug in moments of crisis may be more helpful than an empowering talk by an educator or a professional therapist. The children connect to the support staff because they need the services such staff provides and also because these staff members may remind them of their own parents, and thus create a familiar sense of closeness. Understanding that we have the opportunity to influence people's lives, we should not skip the support staff, who are often behind the scenes and do not always get the chance to celebrate successes.

"To Educate Means to Foster a Sense of Belonging" [40]

In any society, there are young people who do not feel like they belong. They experience alienation due to their ethnic origin, religion or being part of the geographic and social periphery. A teenager who feels disconnected may develop a bubble to live in, as they cultivate aggressive resistance toward society. They do not belong and therefore have nothing to lose. The goal of our educational process is that our graduates become successful adults who contribute to the community. Those who have become accustomed to being alienated are in need of authentic experiences of community. We educators need to develop awareness and guide their sense of belonging. In the third basic principle of the Village Way, we talked about human beings searching for meaning. Within the search for meaning lies the longing of each person to belong to something good, to be part of a group.

Belonging is reinforced by the creation of recurrent rituals, gathering places, symbols, dress, an anthem and a sense of pride. Along with these, we can bolster belonging by enabling people to use their strengths to contribute. Belonging requires hard work. A sense of belonging is expressed in service to the community. In most educational communities, the student is supposed

---

40   S. Yizhar. *On Education and the Education of Values* (Tel Aviv: Am Oved, 1974) N

to receive, and the educator is supposed to give. If we are not careful, we may send the message that the educator is the strong one in the community and only he is there to give, while the student consistently is the needy one and is only there to receive. We should ensure that in the fabric of life in an educational community, the educator and the student both enjoy being in a strong position, as someone who gives of himself to the community, and also occasionally of a vulnerable—even needy—person who allows himself to receive.

The Occasionally Vulnerable Educator

As in many situations in education, here too, this is a delicate situation that should be treated very carefully. A relationship with a student requires a long process of building trust. The pace of attachment is adapted to the needs of the student as he expresses them in his behavior and as they emerge from the routine of educational life. When the educator shares about himself, he needs to be careful to maintain the balance in the teacher-student relationship. This balance is delicate and varies according to the educational situation, the type of encounter and relationship. The supportive educator or adult is not "friends" with the students, but rather, a person who can be trusted and learned from. When a teenager relies on an adult who believes in him, the teen is more likely to believe in himself. Our challenge as educators is to be present in a real way for our students.

I returned exhausted from reserve duty in the IDF after Operation Defensive Shield. The realities of the Operation had begun to sink in— the battles, the various events and the friends who were injured there. I needed time to digest it and recover. In addition to my personal experiences, I had learned that a student of mine had fallen in battle. The grief was deep and the emotional burden heavy. Immediately after the Operation, rumors began about a massacre in Jenin. A public outcry erupted, and international criticism was directed at IDF soldiers. Later, the UN and many other international organizations examined these allegations and found them unequivocally false and baseless, but at the time, the feeling was that we had an accusatory finger pointing right at us, which made the already trying situation even more difficult. That is how I felt when I returned to my class and to the community at Yemin Orde. It was impossible not to share a part of what I felt and experienced. We organized a study evening about moral dilemmas in battle for the entire community and dedicated it in memory of the fallen soldier. With my homeroom class, the situation was harder. It was obvious that I felt weak. The students all knew that I had been called up for reserve duty and they wanted to hear what really happened in Jenin. I felt that I had to share. In such situations, the question of how to share openly and appropriately arises. How does one share in a way that it is real but does not burden the young person, or cross the delicate border that preserves the unique relationship between an educator and a student, between an adult and a teenager? I decided that I would tell my homeroom class what I was going through right then, without elaborating on the experiences of the battle. I told them that I was not at my best, that the Operation was long and difficult, that close friends were hurt, that we had found ourselves in very complex situations, and that I would need time to process everything.

After I shared this with my class, I asked for their help—to take responsibility for several things related to learning and their behavior as a class. I told them in words and deeds that I trusted them, and that I needed them at their best right then. This was an expression of our 'dialogue relationship' alongside my authentic presence. The class came together and took responsibility. It later proved that the connection with this group of students remained special even after they graduated.

In my opinion, what was most crucial was that the young people felt their educator allowed them to express their maturity. It was no longer a one-way connection with the educator giving and the student receiving, but a relationship of reciprocity that recognized the main task of the educator is to educate and the student to be educated, but also allowed the student to experience the role of giver and the educator to accept. In life, we are all occasionally needy or vulnerable and occasionally strong.

A teacher returning from battle is an extreme example. More common examples include a teacher going through a personal or professional crisis, or even needing help with an everyday task.

> *When I switched to using a smartphone, I managed to use it to make calls, but I got into trouble with the world of apps, which felt foreign and inaccessible to me. I decided to ask for help from one of the students. I deliberately chose a student I did not really know apart from class. He was not interested or involved in what was going on in the class. However, it was obvious that he was an app specialist, and that this could be a good start to our relationship. I asked him for help. He didn't understand what I wanted from him, and especially why. I told him honestly that I was struggling. I did not understand anything and needed his help. He sat with me, demonstrated and taught me everything I needed to start working with apps. I said: "Thank you very much, I really needed you."*

This enabled me to experience receiving, and it was a great preparation for the next conversation in which I offered him help and told him, "When I needed you, you gave to me. Now give me a chance to give back." This is a seemingly small but essential step—I really needed help. The student met me in my place of need, where I was ignorant, and he was there for me. At a deeper level, the message was conveyed that no one is perfect. It is worthwhile to ask for help, and it is natural to need the help of another. Even such a small step deepens trust and bolsters the relationship between the student and the educator.

Developing School Spirit at a Last-Chance School

Vocational schools and youth villages are usually labeled as educational or therapeutic frameworks offering students a second, third or last chance. Teens who study in these educational communities may be labeled as "challenging" by parents, teachers and friends. There are youth who study in these communities because they have not met the requirements of the previous framework, and they or their parents recognize that an alternative school is more suitable for their growth. Many of them have diverse strengths that can be expressed in agricultural or vocational education, or in a smaller framework that will enable them to accumulate experiences of success and to leverage them in various fields of knowledge. Because of the labeling, are they less good or less smart? Of course not! But until the experiences of success are internalized, they may be perceived as such by society and, unfortunately, also in their own eyes. In this case, they may feel ashamed and not want others to know that they attend an alternative school, even hiding their school uniform that clearly displays the name of their school.

How do we develop community pride in that situation?

It all begins with each student feeling that people know him, see him and are happy with his presence. This contributes to the quality of the relationships with his friends and educators, and to an internal sense of belonging. The participation of students in various competitions, especially those students that require encouragement, strengthens the image of the educational community. This is even more valid if the team wins, but that is not the main point. Preparation for the competition and interaction with peers from other schools has a positive effect on the student's self-image and sense of belonging. Hosting other students and conducting on-site seminars for teachers from other schools, as well as enabling educational staff to participate in external educational initiatives conveys the message that: "Your school is doing something special which is worthy of studying." Contribution to the community and *Tikkun Olam* activities can also produce school pride, especially when doing so in the public sphere with shirts and flags that represent the educational community.

A public garden in one of the neighborhoods in the town of Hadera was a neglected place frequented by gangs of wandering teens who drank and smoked there. The vegetation, the sidewalks and the facilities conveyed negligence. The social education coordinator of a local Village Way school was busy locating places for Tikkun Olam activities and, at the same time, looking for suitable employment for students who were bumming around during and after school hours. During a conversation with a group of kids, the idea of fixing up the garden in the neighborhood came up. The teacher contacted the city's landscaping department and received a positive response. A short time later, a group of kids arrived with the teacher. Dressed in school shirts and equipped with tools and gloves, they began the work of restoring the garden. On the first day, they surprised the neighborhood residents. On the second day, adults from the neighborhood joined them and asked which school they were from. On the third day and after, neighborhood kids joined the effort; and months later, the garden looked completely different. To celebrate, there was an event for the residents of the neighborhood, and the school's students came in shirts proudly bearing the school logo. The sign at the entrance to the garden bore the name of the school and expressed gratitude to its students.

When a young person receives the message, in speech and actions, that he is part of an educational community rather than 'just another' school, he develops a sense of pride. This begins with a positive feeling that is obvious to others. Later, he may express school pride publicly and wear his uniform, even after school hours.

The Community as a Beacon of Light

When the educational community is consumed only with routine, it furthers the sense of life in survival mode that many of our students bring from previous experiences. The survivor does not have the capacity to pick up his head and look around. So, when a community raises a flag, it allows all students to rally around and develop school pride. We need to identify educational opportunities in which all of us can come together on essential issues. There are many issues that have broad social consent, such as accessibility to people with disabilities, or reducing car accidents. Complex issues that are more hotly debated, such as issues of immigration, refugees, and border control, can also be addressed without fear. Thus, we will be able to inspire involvement, social responsibility and pride at being a part of a community that serves as a source of inspiration, a beacon of light to its surroundings. Above all, it spurs a sense of belonging to a community of meaning in society.

The Square Challenge

The 'four corners of the field,' as depicted in the Village Way roadmap, are a daily challenge. Sometimes they collide and sometimes they conflict with routine life. However, a community that directs its work through the four corners will soon discover that they organize the whole field into one cohesive and dynamic unit. The multitude of people, needs, tasks, characteristics and professions become one continuous educational field. The community is engaged in meaningful content, and each member has a sense of belonging and meaning. Each is an independent entity expressing himself in a dialogical manner. The adults in the community are significant guides, and through their presence, they represent the world of adults for each student. Everyone enriches the educational framework.

We strengthen the center of gravity, the point that promotes growth. Supportive adults and a community of meaning make it possible to best grasp the work of each component of the philosophy. They make the educational space so profound that the 'timeline,' the 'spaceline,' and the circles of *tikkun* can be deepened.

Moments of Grace in Education

The act of education provides many moments of grace for both educator and student. These are moments in which each person has a concrete role, but also the ability to rise above the here and now, to grasp that something significant is taking place. These are moments that create ripples that may turn into waves. The student brings his whole past, his dreams and fears, and interacts with the educator who carries his own past.

Two people meet in one place with all the experiences, feelings and values they have accumulated in their lives—both shared and conflicting ones. Two vulnerable people allow themselves to step out of their usual roles, take down their defenses and be influenced by each other.

This is not the kind of encounter in which the educator directs the student. This is a case in which a different experience must be allowed. It is not a meeting in which one preaches to the other, nor is it a meeting that will be measured by the knowledge acquired by the student. Such meetings are important, but alongside them, we should enable encounters between two people who feel safe and open to accepting what place and time have allowed to bring to fruition. We all have moments in life that we clearly feel are not just another moment. Sometimes we will feel the weight of it while it is taking place, and at times, we will only know later that it was a defining moment in which all the elements of the educational field converged.

Core Principles of Minimizing Institutional Characteristics

The Village Way belief in minimizing institutional characteristics represents the conscious effort to create a community that deviates from the narrow definition of an institution. It seeks to eliminate feelings of alienation, functional uniformity, and bureaucracy inherent in the institution. Institutions in general, especially educational institutions, prefer that life be predictable and under control. A spontaneous flow of life threatens the stability of the institution. But this tendency is contrary to the distinct needs of youth: to feel the flow of life and to be part of a living community that reflects the spirit of its members. Hence the environment should be a place that inspires identification and invites a sense of belonging. This is a difficult, if not paradoxical, task since every educational community is ultimately an institution.

Three Elements of Minimizing Institutional Characteristics:
- **Person:** *Interpersonal connections* between adults and teens which express humanity, caring, respect, and partnership
- **Place:** *Designing the physical environment* in a way that expresses the feeling of home and a warm community
- **Routine:** *Clear, accessible and user-friendly procedures* so that the students and staff understand that every action has a purpose.

Core Principles of Reliable Representations of Parental Wholeness

First and foremost, educators must recognize that a teen's relationship with his parents is irreplaceable. Alongside this, we should form an awareness of the need for complementary parental authority, with educators serving as adult figures of meaning, with the understanding that we never intend to replace parents. Like parents observed by children in different situations, the supportive adult needs to allow the students to see him as a whole person with strengths, weaknesses, and a life story. Stable parenting enables the child to form his identity and serves as a foundation from which he can gain confidence in his abilities. Optimal parenting gives the teen meaning and direction and takes responsibility for the child's existential and emotional needs, as well as imparting values and life skills. Educators should invest in strengthening the relationship of the student with his family, as they work to forge ties between the educational community and the students' families. They must endow the partnership with mutual empowerment, both of parents in the eyes of the child and of the child in the eyes of his or her parents.

Three Elements of Reliable Representations of Parental Wholeness:
- **Three-Dimensional Educator:** A stable, present, accepting, and boundary-setting human figure
- **Strengthening the Parent-Teen Relationship** by empowering the child in the eyes of the parents and empowering the parents in the eyes of the child
- **Strengthening the Educator-Parent Relationship** by getting to know one another and expanding the partnership

Core Principles of Dialogue

It is simpler to conduct oneself in a world that does not require dialogue because unlike real conversations, procedures ensure clarity. Nevertheless, an educator who understands his role as representing parental wholeness will see the ability to open a dialogue as a privilege, not a requirement. Meaningful dialogue indicates to the adolescent that education is an ongoing activity. This is not just a goal we aspire to, but a dynamic process that takes place constantly and recreates itself all the time. In the educational process, there is always room for negotiations contributing to ongoing dialogue. Even when the experience of life is fragmented, the dialogue remains strong and present, allowing opportunities for *Tikkun HaLev* and striving for a life that has meaning and direction.

Dialogue exists not only between the student and significant figures, but between the student and the entire community. Meaningful dialogue can include role-playing exercises that allow both sides to see themselves and find a mooring in calm, measured speech and active listening.

Three Elements of Dialogue:
- **"I-Thou"**: A commitment to getting to know the world of the student who is expressing themselves without blurring the meaningful role of the adult in the conversation
- **Respectful, Growth-Oriented Dialogue** based on **Values-Based Language,** shared among all members of the community
- **One-on-One Conversations:** Every member of the community engages in a dialogue based on mutual respect during a time dedicated for this purpose, along with spontaneous conversations at other times

Core Principles of Community of Meaning

A person is not an isolated island in the world. She realizes her humanity by helping others and working with them. The community is the framework within which a person operates, and through which she gives meaning to action. In community life, the ties between the members are tangible and based in sincerity and humanity. The self-realization of every member of the community depends on these connections, on a sense of belonging. Education does not occur in a bubble. Education demands contact between people, a community spirit. On the way to our higher goal—helping members become leaders of their families and communities—the educational community should allow the teens to experience a sense of collective meaning through ceremonies, celebrations, local customs, common language, gathering places and a common purpose.

A community of meaning is the Village Way term for a community that embodies and publicly expresses the values with which its members identify. The community is a whole that is larger than the sum of its parts, and we believe it has ripples of influence on the larger society around it.

Three Components of Community of Meaning:
- It provides a **sense of belonging** and pride as students build the community
- It promotes a social framework in which all members **help and are helped**, give, and receive
- **The community as a beacon of light:** The members of the community proudly express their collective values and take direct action beyond the borders of the community

CHAPTER 5:

A Whole Philosophy

Different Together

It was December, the first day of the Hebrew month of Kislev at Tel Aviv University, on a particularly stormy night. About a thousand educators who are a part of the Village Way came to a conference on diversity in Israeli culture. In the conference hall, the participants were greeted with quotations on the walls by the great thinkers of human and Israeli history in all their diversity, creating an environment of education and values through words. Circles upon circles of conference participants filled the room, and in every circle, there were people 'being different' together. In every circle, there were unmediated interactions between the many faces of Israeli society, learning together and welcoming one another.

Nadav, an educator wearing a kipah identifying him as an Orthodox Jew, sat in a circle joined by female educators wearing hijabs. In the first round of introductions, there was a palpable tension between the educators of different groups. Nadav was undeterred and tried again. He invited all participating to be open and honest about their discomfort or apprehension. Slowly the Jewish and Arab educators were able to lower their defenses and engage in meaningful discussion of their text study sheets, which contained verses from the Koran and from the Bible, appearing side-by-side.

In a nearby circle, Iyad Salah, the principal of a partner school in Akko which serves the Arab community, led a circle of educators from Jewish communities, who together read texts by John Lennon and David Ben-Gurion. In another circle, a female secular educator led a circle of Orthodox and ultra-Orthodox educators who studied a midrash reflecting the fact that we all have our own different holidays, but the holiday common to all people is celebrating rain. The same rain pours down on us all.

The circles brought together men and women, aged 18–80, from Israel and abroad, from villages, cities and kibbutzim, sabras and immigrants, Arabs and Jews, from the periphery and from the center of the country. For all of them, this was an experience that proved it is possible to be different and be together. All had a common educational mission and a sincere belief that education leads society.

It Takes a Whole Philosophy to Raise a Village

In June, two days before the big event at the end of the school year, we at Yemin Orde would conduct a final formal conversation with the seniors.

What should we say? What is important? Are they listening? We all feel a mixture of joy and fear of separation. We keep the discussion focused. It begins with a question: "Who among the students here has heard the staff say the sentence: "Out of this group, there are great leaders who are going to succeed in life?" All the students in the senior class raise their hands. Now they are asked to close their eyes. "Those who heard this sentence and really believed that the staff meant it personally for you, please raise their hand." Very few hands are raised. They hear the sentence, but they think it is meant for the person next to them, that brilliant student, that good kid. *He came out great, but they don't mean me.*

The staff's eyes meet in confusion, as if they are wondering: "What did we miss? Why don't they believe that we really mean every one of them?" We have 40 minutes to convince them that we do believe in them. But why would it happen now if it has not happened so far? It probably will not happen now, but there is a chance that at this moment, the seeds will be planted to make it happen later. We briefly share experiences of success and positive outcomes. We share challenges that were met with success too, such as a difficult hike that we did not believe we would finish, a test we did not imagine we would pass, and this moment of graduation. All these are 'anchors in our past,' points that combine our personal, family and cultural histories and allow us to properly tell our story, so that it will advance us toward our desired future.

We share experiences of *Tikkun Olam* and what we feel is important to say in terms of values. We do not mention all the important values, but we cannot help but talk about human dignity and the divinity that we can experience when approaching the 'other.'

We thank the parents who trusted us, and we apologize for mistakes we made, partly because of good intentions, and partly because we are human. Let's face it; we also had some difficult moments. We will return to the most authentic place of the human encounter. In conclusion, we tell everyone personally: "When we said that great people would graduate from here, we meant you. You are destined for greatness. The sky is the limit. It's difficult but possible, and we will continue to be here for you."

Adolescence, despite all the difficulties, is essentially a time of grace. Classical psychology would lead us to believe that the decisive age for influencing an individual's emotional and moral structure is early childhood. This is true, but over the years, we have learned from ongoing encounters with students and graduates that we can write more lines in the story during this important stage of life. This is the age of bursting energies that can be directed towards healing, change and growth.

The desire for independence and the signs of rebellion that sometimes characterize this age can cause some to think that there is nothing to do and no one to talk to. Some may regard these as lost years, in which only minor changes can be made in young people whose personality has already been established. We at the Village Way think differently. We have learned that this is a time when tremendous forces are working that can bring about a change in the minds and hearts of adolescents, which could lead to a stronger, safer, more open and accepting society.

The Village Way educational philosophy is multidimensional. It includes the 'earth-sky spaceline,' the 'past-future timeline', 'the corners of the educational field,' and the *tikkun* circles, all of which express the connection between humanity and the world, the ways that both individuals and societies grow. Four corners, two axis and two circles—this is a relatively simple image that works well alongside the natural and professional intuitions of the educator and enables him to define student needs.

The act of education is the human encounter between two people. As King Solomon wrote in *Proverbs*: "As face answers to face in water, so does one man's heart to another."[41] In other words, in human contact there is a reflection. The respect with which I treat the person in front of me is the respect that I will receive in return. Just as my face is reflected in the water, the heart of another will reflect my own heart. How I treat a student or friend is how I will be treated.

This is a nice saying, but in the educational process, many good people have experienced the contrary. A deep sense of frustration and, sometimes, ingratitude accompanies parents and teachers along the way. Therefore, King Solomon chose the imagery of water and not a mirror. A mirror produces an immediate and exact reflection, but to see our reflection in water, we need modesty and patience. We must bow our heads, give up our ego a little, be patient, and wait for the moment when we can see the face reflected in the water. Even then, we discover

---

41 Proverbs 27:19, JPS in Sefaria.com

that the image reflected is blurry. That is, the adolescent will respond to us, but in his own way.

The educational act requires an authentic, professional encounter between the educator and the student, between the community and the individuals who are members of it. The educational act that takes place in an interpersonal encounter is a valuable part, but the value is multiplied and validated when it is carried out within the framework of the 'whole village.' In a community with a common educational philosophy and language, the value of the educational act is greater because it does not stand alone; it exists on a continuum. It combines the many actions of parents, students and educators with agreed-upon values and a common language, with all members assuming a part of the educational responsibility.

The adolescent, like the adults who support him, is searching for meaning. The adults in his life must be professional and authentic, believe in the adolescent and allow him to find that desired meaning. All this is possible if we remember that we are all part of the whole village that is needed to raise a child.

A Story About Searching

Sima and Yaffa were friends, both in the 11th grade at Yemin Orde. Both were high achievers with potential, but they found it difficult to accept authority. If they did not understand the logic or usefulness of a directive, they would not conform. They both lived in a house without a father figure, with mothers and younger siblings. Neither of them returned to school after the Passover holiday. When attempts to contact their mothers failed, the educators were asked to make home visits. The staff went, determined to find out how the girls were. The assumption was that the mothers did not understand the importance of studies for matriculation exams, and perhaps, the young women were assisting their mothers with housework.

The meeting with the mothers was surprising as they, too, were worried because the girls had been missing for about three weeks. We checked with their friends— did the two girls get into trouble with older men? Were they hanging around the sometimes-dangerous Central Bus Station area in south Tel Aviv? We got the same answer from all of them: "I don't know where they are, but you don't have to worry." One of the friends said that they did not want to come back to school, that they were already grown up.

From this thread of a story, we realized that their friends at school were still in touch with them We decided to turn the class into a lesson on mutual responsibility and caring. We discussed the big difference between 'ratting someone out' and sharing information out of concern for them and a desire to save them. During the lesson, there was a tense atmosphere, full of whispers and silences, in which the word Eilat, a popular resort city in Israel, was heard. "Are they in Eilat?" I asked. The response was silence. I implored: "Don't you understand that I'm really worried about them?" No comment. "Don't you understand that their mothers cry, worry and can barely function?" One of the girls said boldly: "I think they are in Eilat. I'm not sure and don't really know where." At once, one of the other girls slapped her, calling her a snitch. "Thank you," I said, and asked the girl who had accused the other of being a snitch to stay after class. In our meeting, I said: "You know where they are. Help us to reassure their mothers. Pick up the phone and talk with them, even if not together with us. " The informal education coordinator and I went into the Village director's office and asked to fly down to Eilat to look for the girls. Our rule is to make every effort to reach the kids, according to our resources and referrals made to the staff.

The director asked, "How likely is it that we will find them if the only information we have is that it is likely they are in Eilat?" True, the odds of finding them were not high but the kids and staff were aware we were going to Eilat to look for them, and that was part of our ongoing effort to prove to the kids that we would never give up on them—not just because it's our job. We felt the message might reach the girls and perhaps they would understand that despite all the difficulties, they could always rely on us to continue the growth process.

When we got to Eilat, we met up with Yaniv, a Village graduate who lived and worked there. He said that he knew they were in town, and he thought they were working at the Princess Hotel. We travelled there, and from a short conversation with a kitchen worker, we learned they worked there in housekeeping. Because they were legally adults of working age, the office refused to share any additional information with us. After a failed search at the hotel, one of the workers told us where they lived. We got to the building but they were not there. After a long wait, we left them two notes, one for each of them:

"Dear Sima / Yaffa: We came all the way here to make sure you are healthy, strong and doing what you choose to do, that you are not being taken advantage of and that no one is hurting you. If you choose to come back, the Village is still open to you. Come back, no questions asked, and we will work hard together to make up what is necessary. If you choose to stay in Eilat, we would be happy to help you however we can, and make sure that your employment contract is fair and that your rights are being protected. In any case, we are on your side. Good luck, and we are waiting for your phone call. Please first contact your moms, then us."

We rushed to catch the flight back. Just then, Yaniv called and said that the girls had promised him that they would talk to us. We decided to wait in Eilat to hear from them and not to get on the return flight. We waited at the entrance to the building when Yaffa came out and said, "You are still here? Don't you guys give up?" This was my first

*conversation with Yaffa. I conveyed the message that we were there
for her, we cared about her and wanted to see her safe, happy, and
putting her abilities to good use. Yaffa said sheepishly that we should
not have come. We asked if she planned to stay or come back, and
she said she had to think about it. Three days later, Yaffa and Sima
called and asked to return to the Village. They returned to a process of
re-absorption, with preparation for 11th grade matriculation exams
and reentering Village life.*

This story clearly shows that the supportive adult and the community
of meaning are primarily responsible for reaching out to the adolescent.
We need to look for a way to make a real encounter. We need to consider
how far we are willing to go to express in action: "We are not giving up on
you. Even if you give up or stop believing in yourself, we believe in you."

Two educators by themselves would have had a much harder time
reaching Yaffa and Sima. But two educators who are part of the 'whole
village' that it takes to raise a child could go down to Eilat, remembering
that Sima and Yaffa are young people searching for meaning. It was
important to say to them in clear, understandable language: You still
belong. Your place in the community is safe.

We went to Eilat to fulfill our educational responsibility and to assist
in the *tikkun* process. Did we go too far? Probably. But this effort is
nothing compared to the pain that Yaffa, Sima, and hundreds of young
people have experienced when adults around them have given up on them.
Considering this reality, maybe we did not go too far at all. This story is
rare, perhaps even once in a lifetime, but hundreds of educators go out
every single day to search for their missing kids. Sometimes, they are
physically searching for them, but most of the time, they are looking for a
way to reach them, a way to their hearts. And unlike a flight to Eilat, this
road cannot be mapped and is much more difficult to travel.

In this book, we have shared the Village Way journey, a voyage
traveled by thousands of committed educators who hold the future of

society in their hands. These dedicated individuals believe that education leads society and are not afraid of the great responsibility placed on their shoulders. They understand that education takes place within the 'whole village,' and that the way to this village is wide enough for everyone to travel together. Within it, each person can find his or her own unique path. All those who share this journey know where they are going, and nevertheless, they understand how important it is to stop, take out a map, and see where they are headed.

www.ingramcontent.com/pod-product-compliance
Lightning Source LLC
Chambersburg PA
CBHW021624120626
46545CB00002B/378